C.S. LEWIS

STARMONT READER'S GUIDE 14
ISSN 0272-7730

BRIAN MURPHY

Series Editor: Roger C. Schlobin

☆ Starmont House ☆
Mercer Island, Washington
1983

Library of Congress Cataloging in Publication Data:

Murphy, Brian.
    C. S. Lewis.

    (Starmont reader's guide ; 14)
    Bibliography: pp. 83-92.
    Includes index.
    1. Lewis, C. S. (Clive Staples), 1898-1963—Criticism and inter-
pretation. I. Title. II. Series.
PR6023.E926Z797 1983   828'.91209   82-7346
ISBN 0-916732-38-X
ISBN 0-916732-37-1 (pbk.)

Second Printing——April, 1984

BRIAN MURPHY is an English professor at Oakland University
in Rochester, Michigan.

CONTENTS

ACKNOWLEDGMENTS AND DEDICATION

It must always be a pleasure to acknowledge the help of one's friends in writing a book, but when the subject of the book is C. S. Lewis, the theme of whose life, it might be said, was friendship, the pleasure is especially fitting. I am particularly grateful to my colleague Donald Morse and to Roger Schlobin who first suggested this project to me, to Joseph DeMent, Dolores Burdick, and Antonia Sanchez for their constant encouragement, and, for help of various kinds, to Ruth Eberle, Kathryn Loeser Farber, William Horwath and Rosalie Murphy. I am especially grateful to Oakland University, its officers and Research Committee members for a Summer Research Grant which gave me time and money to write this book. I dedicate it to my sons John and Mark—who shared so much of the wonderful summer in which it was written.

—Rochester, Michigan

I

CHRONOLOGY

1898	Born, November 29 in Belfast, to Albert James Lewis, an attorney, and Flora Augusta Hamilton Lewis.
1908-14	Educated at various schools in England.
1914-16	Extensive literary and philosophical studies—Latin, Greek, French, German and Italian with wide reading in English—under the private tuition of W. T. Kirkpatrick.
1917	Began studies at Oxford that were interrupted by service in the First World War.
1918	Hospitalized for "trench fever"; rejoined his battalion, wounded, hospitalized again.
1919	Resumed studies at Oxford; published *Spirits in Bondage*, a collection of lyric poems, under the pseudonym of Clive Hamilton.
1924	Established a home near Oxford with Mrs. Jane King Moore, the mother of a slain war-buddy, and her daughter Maureen; later with his brother Warren, an Army officer and expert in seventeenth-century French history.
1925	Elected Fellow of English Language and Literature at Magdalen College, Oxford, where he remained until 1954.
1926	*Dymer*, a book-length narrative poem, also published under the pseudonym of Clive Hamilton.
1929	Converted to Christianity.
1933	*The Pilgrim's Regress: An Allegorical Apology for Christianity, Reason and Romanticism.*
1936	*The Allegory of Love: A Study in Medieval Tradition*, a classic of literary scholarship.

1938	*Out of the Silent Planet*, the first novel in the Space Trilogy.
1939	*The Personal Heresy: A Controversy*, a debate with E. M. W. Tillyard. First met Charles Williams and introduced him to the Inklings, a group which met, usually in Lewis' rooms at Magdalen College, for good talk and mutual criticism of works-in-progress and included, among others, W. H. Lewis, J. R. R. Tolkien, Nevill Coghill, H. V. D. Dyson, A. C. Harwood, C. T. Onions and Robert Havard.
1940	*The Problem of Pain*, his first religious book.
1941	Gave the first of many talks about religion over the BBC.
1942	*The Screwtape Letters*, his most popular book; *A Preface to Paradise Lost*.
1943	*Perelandra*, the second novel in the Space Trilogy; *The Abolition of Man*.
1945	*That Hideous Strength*, the last novel in the Space Trilogy; *The Great Divorce: A Dream*.
1947	*Miracles: A Preliminary Study*.
1950	*The Lion, the Witch and the Wardrobe*, the first of the seven Chronicles of Narnia.
1951	*Prince Caspian*, Narnia Chronicles II.
1952	*The Voyage of the "Dawn Treader,"* Narnia Chronicles III; *Mere Christianity*, his earlier broadcast talks in book form.
1953	*The Silver Chair*, Narnia Chronicles IV.
1954	*The Horse and His Boy*, Narnia Chronicles V; *English Literature in the Sixteenth Century, excluding Drama*, in the Oxford History of English Literature.
1955	Elected Professor of Medieval and Renaissance Literature at Magdalen College, Cambridge. *The Magician's Nephew*, Narnia Chronicles VI; *Surprised by Joy: The Shape of My Early Life*.
1956	*The Last Battle*, Narnia Chronicles VII; *Till We Have Faces: A Myth Retold*.
1956	Married Joy Davidman Gresham.
1958	*Reflections on the Psalms*.
1960	*Studies in Words; The Four Loves*.
1961	*A Grief Observed*, an account of his suffering caused by his wife's death (in 1960), published under the pseudonym of N. W. Clerk; *An Experiment in Criticism*.
1962	*They Asked for a Paper: Papers and Addresses*.
1963	Death, November 22.

II

INTRODUCTION: "Soft Dreams Filled with Promise"

C. S. Lewis was a contentious man. He believed in argument, in disputation, and in the dialectic of Reason because he believed that the main business of life was a bold hunt for truth. Consequently, he was contentious, and he was strongly assertive. Indeed, as a small child who (rather understandably) disliked his given names of Clive Staples, he presented himself before his mother, pointed a finger at himself, and announced, "He is Jacksie." And so, for the rest of his life, on the basis of a decision he had taken at the age of three or four, he remained "C. S." to the world but "Jack" to the private world of his close friends he so loved.

Lewis seemed always to take himself seriously, calmly; in his twenties he knew himself: "I think I know my own limitations and am quite sure that an academic and literary career is the only one in which I can go beyond the meanest mediocrity" (*Letters*, p. 82. All citations are to the works listed in the bibliographies). An ambitious and serious young man, he worked hard, even battled, to become an Oxford don. But he was a writer; and, early on, he assumed that the "literary" part of his career would be poetry: his first two books were verse, a collection of lyrics and a long narrative poem. But Lewis happened to be on the wrong, the losing, side in one of history's wars of literary fashion. By the time Lewis had just begun as a poet, his kind of poetry was already finished. As his great friend Nevill Coghill said, "In those early twenties, before the victories of the New Sensibilities had become certain, Masefieldian romance and narrative manner were still appreciated, though the half-lyrical, half-elegiac and very fragmentary contemplations that compose *The Waste Land* had already appeared and were establishing a very different kind of

11

English'' (*Light on C. S. Lewis*, pp 58-59).

While the strange new sounds and images of "patients being etherized upon a table" from "Prufrock" created Modernism, Lewis was writing gentle, traditional, and rather beautiful verse like this:

> Today was all unlike another day.
> The long waves of my sleep near morning broke
> On happier beaches, tumbling lighted spray
> Of soft dreams filled with promise. As I woke,
> Like a huge bird, Joy with the feathery stroke
> Of strange wings brushed me over. Sweeter air
> Came never from dawn's heart. The misty smoke
> Cooked it upon the hills. It touched the lair
> Of each wild thing and woke the wet flowers everywhere
> (Green and Hooper, *Biography*, p. 79).

But there was simply no longer an audience for the kind of lyrical, romantic, and meditative poetry he wanted to write.

However, Lewis, that contentious man, would not give up. He spent the rest of his fruitful life writing an astonishingly diverse, richly variegated, apparently quite reserved, even sober, series of books, articles, essays, lectures, and even sermons— through all of which, almost without exception, there runs, like a thin vein of gold, the rich and deep lyric beauty that we call poetry.

In his own lifetime, Lewis acquired at least four devoted but apparently quite discrete audiences. Scholars, critics and students respected Lewis as one of the scholarly luminaries of his time: *The Allegory of Love* remains a major study and a powerful work of imaginative scholarship, a work which shapes our sense of medieval love poetry, of Courtly Love, and even the Middle Ages generally; *The Discarded Image* is a brilliant introduction to Medieval and Renaissance literature; and Lewis' volume in *The Oxford History of English Literature* is literary history at its most magisterial.

Only two years after *The Allegory of Love*, his first major book, Lewis published the first of his religious books. In *The Problem of Pain*, he dealt with the most difficult of theological problems— reconciling a good God with His created world of evil and suffering. The book opens with a remarkably lucid account of Lewis' own earlier atheism; so the opening pages comprise a brilliant statement of a specially modern and mournful kind of materialism, and it is with this philosophic position that the rest of the book, so to speak, does battle. With a wit, charm, humor, a razor-keen mind and his contentious mode of discourse, he wrote, in effect, one of the clearest, most honest, and most moving religious statements ever penned. For it is a religious statement, a kind of *confessio*, as well as a brilliant case for Christianity. It is so simple a book in form and design that a reader might miss the fact that it is also an arrestingly original way of talking about religion. His originality—which he always vigorously denied—became obvious enough with *The Screwtape Letters* and the even more absorbing *Great Divorce*. Religious believers as well as nonbelievers found something unique, something invaluable and irreplaceable in Lewis' work: a unique combination of a rigorously logical, philosophically taut exposition with a coolly objective, personal *apologia*.

The third and fourth audiences were readers of his fiction. He called his Space Trilogy—*Out of the Silent Planet, Perelandra,* and *That Hideous Strength*—a "kind of theologized science fiction" (*Letters*, p. 260). His fourth novel, his least-read work, *Till We Have Faces*, is a very complex and dense re-telling of the Psyche and Eros myth. His fourth audience is probably his most devoted, certainly the most joyously uncritical and grateful—the children who have made *The Chronicles of Narnia* one of the handful of genuine children's classics of the twentieth century, possibly of all time.

Since Lewis' death in 1963, and especially in the 1970s, his four audiences have grown, so to speak, more acquainted with each other. What they find is a remarkable unity of tone and spirit in all these quite different works. Lewis said it himself when he described "the guiding thread" in a "very mixed bag" of his books. The "guiding thread" is what I have called the vein of gold. Sometimes that vein can be seen quite easily. It is, of course, the verse he only very rarely permitted himself to write. Consider this conclusion to his study *Miracles*:

> These small and perishable bodies we now have were given to us as ponies are given to schoolboys. We must learn to manage: not that we may some day be free of horses altogether but that some day we may ride bareback, confident and rejoicing, those greater mounts, those winged, shining and world-shaking horses which perhaps even now expect us with impatience, pawing and snorting in the King's stables.

It is less surprising that Lewis the religious writer should become "poetic" than it is that his critical work should, rather more subtly, modulate from his splendidly workmanlike prose (written, it would seem, to Orwell's fine ideal that good prose should be like a windowpane) to the highly charged images of his poetic prose. Here is a passage describing Shakespeare's Sonnets:

> Thus from extreme particularity there is a road to the highest universality. The love is, in the end, so simply and entirely love that our *cadres* are thrown away and we cease to ask what kind. However it may have been with Shakespeare in his daily life, the greatest of the sonnets are written from a region in which love abandons all claims and flowers into charity: after that it makes little odds what the root was like. They open a new world of love poetry; as new as Dante's and Petrarch's, had been in their day. These had of course expressed humility, but it had been the humility of Eros hungry to receive: kneeling, but kneeling to ask. (*English Literature of the Sixteenth Century*, p. 505)

But, beautiful, powerful and irreplaceable as these golden passages are for us, they were not sufficient for Lewis. He had not wanted merely to write Romantic poetry; he wanted to write romances. But in the 1930s there were no romances to write. (We can now see how inevitable it was that Lewis should have written later in his life his romances in the form of children's stories; he would probably have said that he was not yet old enough to write them in the 1930s.) Serious writers like Graham Green, scholars like Lewis' friend Dorothy Sayers might write detective stories as acceptable *bagatelles*, and a Hemingway might be free to admire a Simenon. But if in the 1930s a serious writer wanted to write a science-fiction novel, he might have accomplished his professional purpose more quickly by simply cutting his throat. Hemingway records that he was embarrassed by, and Fitzgerald apologized for, the dust-jacket of the first edition of *The Great Gatsby* because it looked like "bad science fiction"— and that, presumably, is the worst there is (*A Moveable Feast*, p. 176). Science ficiton was low, weird, *outre*, pulpy.

It is one more indication of Lewis' contentiousness that he elected to write one of these pulpy and absurd things, to model it on H. G. Wells' space stories and David Lindsay's *Voyage to Arcturus*, and to give it the rather lurid title *Out of the Silent Planet*.

One might expect Lewis to have been castigated by his colleagues and the "mainstream" critics: he was; or, he would have been if anyone had bothered to notice very much. Lewis might have been quite justified in thinking, in the immortal phrase of

Oliver Goldsmith, that the public *made a point* of not knowing anything he published. But now? Surely Lewis is revered as one of the pioneers of modern science fiction, now that it is at last enjoying attention and respect.

However, the case of Lewis in the modern world of science-fiction letters is somewhat strange. He enjoys respect but little attention. For example, in an excellent summary of the state of the art, *Science Fiction Today and Tomorrow* (ed. Reginald Bretnor [Baltimore: Penguin Books, 1974]), Lewis is referred to as one of "the true giants of science fiction" along with such classic worthies as H. G. Wells and Olaf Stapledon. The surprise is that while Wells, not surprisingly, receives no fewer than thirty references in the book, Lewis receives exactly one.

It might be countered that Lewis is more a fantasist than science-fiction writer; there is some truth in the argument—certainly his novels from *That Hideous Strength* on are fantasies. But the first two novels of his trilogy are surely classic voyage-to-outer-space examples of pure science fiction. Lewis' somewhat uneasy position as a neglected "true giant" is instructive however—both as to science fiction generally and Lewis' novels in particular.

A brilliant essay by James Gunn, "Science Fiction and the Mainstream," makes clear the proposition that science fiction is not only a literary form but also a kind of loosely held philosophy. What makes Lewis something of a critical pariah is that while he wrote two formally brilliant science-fiction novels, his values do not seem compatible with the philosophy of science fiction.

One basic division among thoughtful people might be summarized as follows: there are those who think our destiny is within ourselves, those who think it without, and those who think we have no destiny. Lewis (like many fantasists) is among the first, and most science-fiction writers are found among the second—often chosen as an uneasy alternative to the third. Ultimately, it is a question of value. While Lewis himself liked science fiction—he loved the early Wells novels and hailed joyously the appearance of so obviously great a science-fiction novel as Arthur C. Clarke's *Childhood's End*—he must surely have been aware that his values were quite different from most science-fiction writers; he merely shared with them a good many opinions.

James Gunn's summary of one essential philosophical science fiction position is crucial: "The farther into space one travels the less significant become the passions and agonies of man, and the only matter of importance in the long morning of man's struggle to survive is his survival so that his sons could be seeded among the stars" (In *Science Fiction Today and Tomorrow*, p.

199). This comes very close to being what Lewis called "Westonism" and represents the very philosophy he was attacking through the whole of his Space Trilogy. He began to write *Out of the Silent Planet* precisely because he was appalled, as he said, by "the realization that thousands of people in one way and another depend on some hope of perpetuating and improving the human race for the whole meaning of the universe" (*Letters*, p. 167).

Lewis would certainly reverse James Gunn's sentence and would say: The farther into space one travels, the *more* significant become the passions and agonies of man. Lewis' science-fiction novels (as well as his later fantasies) offer something very special, then: they offer an examination of the whole question of value. In effect Lewis argues that science-fiction writers simply assume the value of survival quite apart from any particular, examined value in whatever survives. In all of Lewis' work, value itself is evaluated.

III

LEWIS THE MAN, THE MAIN OUTLINES

C.S. Lewis hardly knew his mother, who died of cancer when he was nine. He had an extremely difficult, at times even tense, relationship with his father. However, with his only brother, Warren, he shared a fraternal love which, although disturbed at the end of his life, became the emotional rock on which C. S. Lewis built the foundations of his private life.

The merely exasperating side of his relationship with his father is wittily and movingly given in *Surprised by Joy* (a book which is, arguably but certainly possibly, the greatest autobiography of the twentieth century). Lewis explains that his father "sometimes appeared not so much incapable of understanding anything as determined to misunderstand everything" (*Surprised by Joy*, p. 123). "Tell him that a boy called Churchwood had caught a field mouse and kept it as a pet, and a year, or ten years later, he would ask you, 'Did you ever hear what became of poor Chickweed who was so afraid of the rats?' " (p. 121). His father's determination to be a pal to his sons proved to be extremely exhausting to the brothers, no matter what their age: as children they roamed the large house with its many interesting rooms—always until their father returned at which time they would cease to talk or read or play and would be forced by their always (and no doubt horrifyingly) well-intentioned father to engage in what he fondly imagined was conversation. The effect of such conversation, amusing at a distance is really profound:

> The hours my father spent at home were thus hours of perplexity for us boys. After an evening of the sort of conversation I have been describing one felt as if one's head were spinning like a top. His presence put an end

to all our innocent as well as to all our forbidden occupations. It is a hard thing—nay, a wicked thing—when a man is felt to be an intruder in his own house. And yet, as Johnson said, "Sensation is sensation" (*Surprised by Joy*, p. 123).

Lewis described his reading of George Macdonald's *Phantastes* at the age of sixteen as one of the great revelations of his life and the author as his lifelong guide. *The Great Divorce*, a religious fantasy in the form of a dream-vision, pays tribute to MacDonald by making him Lewis' Virgil, his guide through the Underworld. Lewis' description of MacDonald's life is particularly moving, therefore, when one knows something of Lewis' sense of emotional deprivation and alienation:

> An almost perfect relationship with his father was the earthly root of all his wisdom. From his own father, he said, he first learned that Fatherhood must be at the core of the universe. He was thus prepared in an unusual way to teach that religion in which the relation of Father and Son is of all relations the most central (*George MacDonald: An Anthology*, p. 10).

The decidedly imperfect relationship Lewis shared with his own father was, of course, also one of the roots of his life. Lewis felt, he said, like "an intruder in his own house," and that meant he must establish his own house, his own life with, perhaps, at the least an absence of the emotional turmoil and confusion that he had experienced as a boy and an adolescent.

So, in one way, Lewis' life was almost perfectly predictable. Always a passionate reader, he and his teachers knew that a literary education and an academic career were his destiny. He was a brilliant pupil (except for mathematics) and made a sufficient reputation at Oxford to be awarded a much-prized Fellowship. As a Fellow he lived most of his life in a quiet routine of lectures, tutorials and writing. He often said that he liked monotony—meaning, of course, that he liked the quiet and regular rhythms of the academic life with its time to teach and its time to read and its time to write.

Thus, to most of his readers, Lewis was a don, a pipe-smoking, clubbable man who was devoted to his friends and who took long walks through the Oxfordshire lanes and wrote a great number of valuable books: withal, a charming, pleasant, witty man.

But an alert reading of Lewis' fiction makes clear what lies just below the surface of all his work. The surface is beautiful, organized, gloriously rational—for no modern writer believed in Reason with the ferocious decisiveness Lewis did. However, just below that surface is something restless, even at times brooding, seething with passion.

The clue is knowing what it means to be "an intruder in his own house." There was so much that he felt, so much that he wanted to share. He had felt "the feathery stroke / Of strange wings," and he had dreamed "soft dreams filled with promise"; he had known the Joy, the ecstasy of both the natural world's "splendour in the grass" and the ache of his own soul, the longings of his heart. The theme of *Surprised by Joy* is his learning of this Joy, his losing it, his futile attempts to find or revive it until he learned that one had, exactly, to be surprised by this Joy as one did other things, as one found God. His first book was titled *Spirits in Bondage*, and the title itself describes Lewis' sense of things and himself at that time: he was in bondage; much of his life and all of his novels are concerned with the freeing of the spirit.

His early life was dominated by two kinds of progress, rational and mystical. But Lewis tended to distrust the mystical—in himself and in others—perhaps because he thought of the mystical as a kind of alternative to Reason. In fact, his "Reason" included the mystical. His famous account of his conversion suggests this. "Doubtless, by definition," he wrote, "God was Reason itself." This was the summation, the point, the object of that Reason he had studied for so long and with such delight: he loved the clean, bracing, impersonal, honest and objective logic of his tutor Kirkpatrick because it was important. Philosophy, he knew, was not a mere "subject": it was a search for wisdom; he tried to live his philosophy.

But when he came to the source of light, there was no light but darkness:

> Doubtless, by definition, God was Reason itself. But would He also be "reasonable" in that other, more comfortable, sense? Not the slightest assurance on that score was offered me. Total surrender, the absolute leap in the dark, were demanded.

Then comes this famous passage:

> You must picture me alone in the room in Magdalen, night after night, feeling, whenever my mind lifted even for a second from my work, the steady, unrelenting approach of Him whom I so earnestly desired not to

19

meet. That which I greatly feared had at last come upon me. In the Trinity Term of 1929 I gave in, and admitted that God was God, and knelt and prayed: perhaps, that night, the most dejected and reluctant convert in all England (*Surprised by Joy*, pp. 228-29).

Lewis asks us to picture him at work "night after night." Why not day after day? He was, in many senses, "one acquainted with the night"; and it was an acquaintanceship that affected all his work. For one thing, it surely was the motive power behind his drive to "defend" his religion. Always combative and assertive, he attended church long before he was really a Christian, as opposed to a theist, because, he said, he felt one ought to "fly one's flag" (*Surprised by Joy*, p. 233). And after the Christian Church seemed not merely logically tenable, but logically inescapable and therefore morally compelling, he began writing his series of religious books, only two of which (*Reflections on the Psalms* and *Letters to Malcolm*) are not apologetics—reasoned defenses of Christianity and persuasive arguments which have helped to convert untold numbers of people, for Lewis has become a major force in Christianity in our time, and he holds a position really quite unlike one ever held by anyone at any time. One must go back to the time of Cardinal Newman and the Oxford Movement to find a religious writer with Lewis' impact, but even Newman was one among many influential Victorian religious writers.

His religious books are so good, so beautifully written and soundly argued, that they will surely stand, in the English-speaking world, for a generation or more as the fundamental statement of basic (or "mere") Christianity. And yet, Lewis confessed that no religious doctrine seemed more remote to him than one he had just successfully "defended" (*Letters*, p. 209). It was as if a circle developed in which he would feel the truth ("sensation is sensation," as he was fond of quoting), doubt, then rationally defend, again doubt and then feel the truth again. Lewis' religious books are uniquely valuable because of the strength of the emotional foundation which, though unseen, supports his rational structure.

His biographers tell us, "Lewis in fact learnt of love as he learnt to love" (Green and Hooper, p. 267). Like Browning's Grammarian, Lewis refused to leave mere learning for something called "life": "Actual life comes next? / Patience a moment." Browning said of his Grammarian that "This man decided not to Live but Know." For Lewis, living and learning were constant and constantly reciprocal.

In the matter of sex, for example (and it was about love that the biographers were speaking), Lewis was—as he had a perfect right to be, as do we all—very private in his own life. Sexual experience, as part of the pursuit of Joy, hinted at in *Surprised by Joy* and more explicit in *The Pilgrim's Regress*, was clearly part of his early life.

One of the more mysterious chapters in Lewis' life began just after he left the Army and returned to Oxford. He began living with the mother (and her daughter) of a friend of his, Paddy Moore, who had been killed in the war. His brother suggests that he turned to Mrs. Moore as a second mother because of the breach between him and his father and because of "some war-time promise made to Paddy Moore" (*Letters*, p. 12).

There was clearly more to it: Lewis was a passionate young man, eager to love—his early letters to his bosom friend Arthur Greeves (his first friend, and one with whom he corresponded all his life) describe his attractions and attachments; he had sampled love and sex in the normal adolescent ways. But two factors seemed almost to have arrested the progress of this side of his emotional life. The first was his aversion to homosexuality, which (at least as he found it widely practiced in the schools he attended where it was, in effect, pederasty) so nauseated him that he distrusted all "the lusts of the flesh."

The second was his relationship with Mrs. Moore. He referred to it only very darkly (another acquaintance with the night) in *Surprised by Joy*. There is no way of knowing exactly the nature of Lewis' and Mrs. Moore's relationship, and, in many ways, it does not matter now: we can see fairly clearly the results of it. Lewis obviously loved her, and when his father found out about her, it is clear that he regarded it as an amorous entanglement: "All I know about the lady," he piteously complained, "is that she is old enough to be his mother" (Green and Hooper, *Biography*, p. 62). One does not point out that a mother-substitute is old enough to be a mother. In any case, Lewis described Arthur Greeves and Mrs. Moore as the people who meant more to him than all others.

No matter if Lewis' feelings for Mrs. Moore were a combination of the filial, the erotic, the affectionate, and even the dutiful; the fact is the love quickly died, and for the rest of Mrs. Moore's life, Lewis felt an obligation to her that seemed to preclude the possibility of ordinary love.

It is one of the more curious coincidences that Lewis, who has been so often compared to Dr. Johnson, should have been like Johnson even in his emotional and domestic life. Like Johnson, Lewis loved a much older woman. And, again like Johnson, Lewis maintained a household that was quarrelsome and given to constant domestic and emotional crises. Small wonder Johnson took to the taverns as Lewis kept to his rooms in college, and both surrounded themselves with talkative, argumentative, and good-natured male friends.

After Mrs. Moore's death, Lewis, apparently now feeling free to do so, fell in love and married Joy Davidman Gresham. But even that relationship was marked by Lewis' wariness: they were first married in a civil ceremony intended only as a legal means of allowing Joy, an American, to stay in Britain. But eventually he allowed himself to love her, and Nevill Coghill has recalled Lewis' touching sentence, uttered as he and Coghill watched Joy walk toward them, "I never expected to have, in my sixties, the happiness that passed me by in my twenties" (*Light on C. S. Lewis*, p. 63).

Between the time he began living with Mrs. Moore, in 1918, and her death in 1951—that is, most of Lewis' adult life—his emotional life was determined by his duty to Mrs. Moore. This had two principal effects: one on his life, the other on his work. The effect on his life was his turning to male friendships, most especially with his brother (a process begun by his emotionally thwarted relationship with his father).

Lewis had such strong friendships with men that they recall the great male friendships of a feudal, even pre-feudal, society. Lewis' love for his brother is infused with warmth and strength, and the whole of their relationship was, as they recognized, cyclical: they began as small boys, allies against the adult world; later as allies against the schools, as comrades-in-arms in the First World War; separated, they wrote each other regularly; together, they created a home; and in Lewis' last illness they were, as Major Lewis said, "together in the little end room at home," where they would recapture "the old schoolboy technique of extracting the last drop of juice from our holidays," and in the end, C. S. Lewis died in his brother's arms (*Letters*, p. 25).

A secure and emotionally solid relationship with his brother was the pattern. It was a pattern Lewis was able fortunately to weave into other close friendships. Like Dr. Johnson, Lewis believed in friendship, and believed, as Johnson said, in keeping his friendships "in good repair." Also like Dr. Johnson, Lewis formed a very loose literary club, The Inklings, described accurately by Major Lewis as "a famous and heroic gathering, one that has already passed into literary legend"—and one that, as time goes on, will pass into literary history (*Letters*, p. 13).

It would be hard to over-estimate the role of male friendship in Lewis' life: Arthur Greeves, his brother, Owen Barfield, Charles Williams, these men Lewis loved with a kind of love rarely found in the literary anecdotes of our time and were possible to him because of a special combination of temperament and personal history.

Until the moment, however, when he could talk to Nevill Coghill about the happiness that had passed him by in his twenties, Lewis paid a price for the emotional dam that his life with Mrs. Moore created. In matters of sex and romance, Lewis affected a kind of huffiness, an air, sometimes, of amused condescension toward those whose lives might be disturbed by something so *emotional* as erotic love. It goes almost without saying that his correspondingly defensive sense of lofty male superiority is one of the least attractive aspects of his character. The following astonishing assertion shows, to say the least, an imperfect awareness of sexual psychology: "The idea of female beauty is the erotic stimulus for women as well as men . . . i.e., a lascivious man thinks about women's bodies, a lascivious woman thinks about her own. *What* a world we live in!" (*Letters*, p.141). Lewis' use of "lascivious" is perhaps even more revealing than the substance of his statement.

In his expository, particularly religious, work, Lewis' guarded attitude sometimes shows itself as simply excessively careful, sometimes excessively concerned to be un-modern; Lewis himself recognized this danger: "I am conscious," he said, "of a partly pathological hostility to what is fashionable" (*Letters*, p. 179). "Liberated" sexual attitudes were not only un-Christian; they were fashionable. Always fond of stating clearly the Christian attitude toward sex as being acceptable only in marriage, Lewis put a remarkable sentence into the mouth of his devil Screwtape: "The Enemy's demand on humans takes the form of a dilemma; *either* complete abstinence *or* unmitigated monogamy" (*The Screwtape Letters*, p. 80). Lewis obviously means this to be a plain, blunt statement of the Christian position on sex. But observe: abstinence or monogamy comprise a dilemma, and a dilemma—as so careful a man with words as Lewis would surely know—is a choice between equally balanced and therefore equally unsatisfactory choices. Thus, "dilemma" must surely be a slip— an impression reinforced by the connotations of the word "unmitigated."

But Lewis "learnt of love as he learnt to love," and after his love for Joy, his attitude can be seen changed in a work like *The Four Loves* and, luminously, in *Till We Have Faces.*

It is worth dwelling at some length on Lewis' emotional life because it shows a man quite different from the usual portrait— the witty, amusing, lofty don who seemed to have all the answers to life and few of the problems (the portrait of his admirers) or else the complacent, smug, male-supremacist reactionary with a gift of gab (the portrait of his detractors). He was a more complex and more profound man, more deeply affected by the sheer intensity of life—whose passions and problems were the stuff out of which he created his work.

It is also worth understanding Lewis the man because it is the easier to come to a juster appreciation of his work, particularly his poetry and fiction, and thus, indirectly, to a clearer understanding of his place in literary history. For one thing, Lewis as a writer is almost as remarkable for what he did not write about as what he did. He wrote very little about sex and about romantic love—except for *Till We Have Faces*, a book which is fully understandable only in terms of Lewis' development.

As Lewis grows increasingly important in literary history, it becomes clear that he brought something to modern letters quite different from anything brought by his contemporaries. If Camus had never written *The Stranger* or Hemingway *A Farewell to Arms*, we could nonetheless easily, in intellectual history, reconstruct the importance of the theme of the alienated man, the rebel, the outsider. But without Lewis there would have been a hole, an absence not only of a development of a kind of religious psychology, a regenerative or restated Christianity, but of a fiction which treats of the relation between the soul and the self in a unique way.

IV

A "KIND OF MADNESS" ON A "SILENT PLANET"

The initial "complication" of *Out of the Silent Planet* is a kidnapping: two men, both academicians, kidnap a forty-year-old Cambridge philologist named Ransom—the obvious point of the name being that he is his own Ransom, that nothing can buy him off, that only he—although chosen fortuitously, now that the choice is accomplished—will do.

When Ransom finds himself on a space ship heading into Outer Space, he, not unnaturally, wants to know how the ship is powered. One of his captors, Weston, a physicist, says, "If it makes you happy to repeat words that don't mean anything—which is, in fact, what unscientific people want when they ask for an explanation—you may say we work by exploiting the less observed properties of solar radiation" (pp 26-27).

So much for "science"; Weston's gruff brevity is, in this case, the author's own. A reader of science fiction who delights in technical detail and scientific speculation had better pass on at once. What interests Lewis is what-would-happen-if; he imagines a space ship traveling to Mars and hasn't the slightest interest in how it might get there.

Once there . . . that is another story; in fact, the story Lewis wrote. His imagination is primarily visual: a lunar landscape, the purple forests of Malacandra, those are the kinds of things that interested, or rather seized, him—not technology. "All my seven Narnian books, and my three science fiction books, began with seeing pictures in my head," Lewis explained. "At first, they were not a story, just pictures. The *Lion* all began with a picture of a Faun carrying an umbrella and parcels in a snowy wood. This picture had been in my mind since I was about sixteen" (*Of Other Worlds*, p. 42). Anyone who has read through the trilogy would know this, would remember the ancient forests of Malacandra, the voluptuously floating islands of Perelandra, the image of Mr. Bultitude in *That Hideous Strength*. Lewis as a child wrote a series of stories with his brother about a mythical country called Boxen: to the adult Lewis, then, science fiction offered the obvious means to explore his talent for and delight in the creation of his own landscapes, his own worlds. Some of the images he has created, like the Green Woman on her floating island, have an oddly uncanny power to stay in the reader's mind quite apart from what these images might "mean" or be used for.

Almost as the rational Lewis was driven to defend the religious faith he felt the truth of, so Lewis the novelist used his images, his picture, to develop fairly clearly worked out propositions. What Lewis meant the informing idea behind *Out of the Silent Planet* to be is clear from the letter he wrote not long after the book was published: "What set me about writing the book was the discovery that a pupil of mine took all that dream of interplanetary colonization quite seriously, and the realization that thousands of people in one way and another depend on some hope of perpetuating and improving the human race for the whole meaning of the universe—that a 'scientific' hope of defeating death is a real rival to Christianity" (*Letters*, p. 167). This is the "danger of 'Westonism,' " which Lewis took "to be real."

So Lewis shares with any science-fiction writer a concern with human destiny and the stars, a desire to know our place in the scheme of things, and the hope that something of that meaning can be wrested from the galaxies by means of intuition and imagination. The great difference is that Lewis, so to speak, takes an already coherent philosophy with him as he begins his journey.

Lewis dedicated the novel to his brother and makes a bow in the direction of H. G. Wells: Lewis' sources are not hard to find, but it is somewhat more difficult to judge just what use he made of those sources, Wells, David Lindsay's *Voyage to Arcturus*—these are in the immediate background.

However, Lewis was not using any particular work as a formal or philosophical pattern. It is easy to say that "Christianity" lies behind *Out of the Silent Planet*, and all of the trilogy—and, indeed, all of Lewis. But the question is: whose Christianity? which Christianity? Of course, the core is certainly there: man's "fall" or rejection of the abundant life offered by God and consequent need for redemption, by means of a divine and human agent, for a restoration to that life. But the basis for the Christian "matter" on which art can be based extends far beyond even the rich variety of stories and characters from the Bible. We must

26

beware even of citing *Paradise Lost*: Bernard Shaw's great third act of *Man and Superman* contains the Devil's amusing complaint that he and his domain have been misunderstood and misreported—especially by Dante and Milton:

> The Italian described it as a place of mud, frost, filth, fire, and venomous serpents: all torture. This ass, when he was not lying about me, was maundering about some woman whom he saw once in the street. The Englishman described me as being expelled from Heaven by cannon and gunpowder; and to this day every Briton believes that the whole of his silly story is in the Bible.

This "silly story"—that is, about Satan's waging a battle with the Heavenly forces—is not in the Bible. It is part of the pool of stories about Jesus, the saints, the martyrs, including filigrees on the Old Testament stories, which comprises the legends and traditions of Christianity.

Lewis, for his trilogy, is willing to draw from any of that material. Indeed, one of the most remarkable aspects of his work is his attempt to find the grain of truth in even the most fanciful of these stories: it becomes even clearer in *Perelandra* in which Lewis tries to use whatever mythologies and legends that might conceivably shed light on man's moral origins.

The cosmic and individual, the macro and microcosmos, the world and the soul, society and the individual: Lewis' trilogy constantly moves in and out, from great to small, seeking "a world in a grain of sand" and keeping fairly close track of the actual grains of sand at the same time. Lewis once remarked that the two poems he turned to most often were *The Prelude* and the *Aeneid* (*Letters*, p. 228). The high, heroic world of the *Aeneid* is obviously mirrored in Lewis' concern with the origins of things, with the intricate and delicate ways small actions connect with momentous events in a subtle circuit of destiny and free will. But Wordsworth's *Prelude* is also to be seen in Lewis—in the quest for self-knowledge and self-realization through Nature.

Of course, both the *Aeneid* and *The Prelude* are tales of journeys: Wordsworth's walks, Aeneas' long quest for Rome are the narrative frames which Lewis had in his bones. *Out of the Silent Planet* has two journeys, one within the other. It is an important point for the structural balance of the novel: Ransom wants only a little holiday walking tour by himself: this is interrupted by a trip to Malacandra (Mars), and the narrative part of the novel ends with a spendidly controlled anticlimax in which Ransom leaves the space ship. "He had seen dim lights, the lights of men . . . . A lighted door was open . . . . He pushed his way in, regardless of the surprise he was creating and walked to the bar. 'A pint of bitter, please,' said Ransom" (p. 151).

So Lewis' hero concludes his travels to Mars with a glass of beer in an English pub! This is characteristic of Lewis: to insist on the body's necessities and pleasures—no matter if the context is a religious crisis or a space trip. It is also appropriate that Lewis frames the greater voyage within the smaller.

The moral significance of the book is almost entirely contained in the first chapter, rightly understood. Ransom is first introduced as "The Pedestrian," a traveler without any particular individuality; it is significant that Lewis gives us no background—and it would have been an easy temptation for Lewis to indulge himself, especially in his first novel, with an elaborate description of one of those walking tours he so loved, perhaps even preceded by an account of how Ransom left Cambridge, notes on Cambridge life, and so forth.

But Lewis' whole approach to his character is the key to his understanding of personality. Ransom is The Pedestrian, a Walker, Nobody in Particular—that is, more Anybody than Everyman. The distinction is important: Ransom is not a summation of essential human characteristics, like the Everyman of the great morality play; rather, he merely happens to be a Cambridge philologist, aged around forty or so, tallish but with a scholarly stoop, and, although he is a conventionally religious man, we learn remarkably little about Ransom's mind or soul. Lewis gives us a very particular, but not profound, character with a particular set of virtues and vices. He certainly is not "born great," and he "achieves greatness" (eventually) only by the way he responds to the particular opportunity for the greatness which happens to be "thrust upon" him.

The opportunity for the "greatness" is given to Ransom because of a particular set of circumstances, none of them very remarkable in themselves. But even the basic condition, that Ransom is alone (and is thus abductable) quietly sets up a condition to which Lewis will often allude: all his characters, from Ransom at the beginning to Mark and Jane Studdock at the end, all want to be alone, all desire to call their souls their own. But, in Lewis' world, no one belongs to himself; Ransom cannot "ransom" himself.

Ransom discovers that he belongs to forces far beyond anything he ever imagined at first because of the simplest of human obligations. Nearly lost on his walking tour (and even the map is worth a point, for in Lewis' world, there are guides, but they are frequently fallible and, in any case, the world of the guide is often undercut by purely human agency—as evidenced by the landlady who refused Ransom a room at an inn), Ransom must ask directions of a woman worried because her retarded son is late coming home from work. The woman explains that her son works for a "professor" and "a gentleman from London." Ransom sees that the woman is very worried about her son. Then comes a characteristically Lewisan sentence: "It occurred to him that he ought to call on the mysterious professor and ask for the boy to be sent home: and it occurred to him just a fraction of a second later that once he were inside the house—among men of his own profession—he might very reasonably accept the offer of a night's hospitality" (p. 9). It is the crucial "fraction of a second" that we notice in Lewis; he always sorts out his characters' motives meticulously—though not primarily in a psychological way. Rather, he offers a kind of psychological pattern within which decisions are made and actions taken. It certainly affects our judgment of Ransom to know that he thought first of the worried woman and then of his tired self.

Graham Greene is another major British novelist who deals in these crucial fractions of seconds, but the aesthetic effect is rather different. In *Brighton Rock*, for instance, one phrase is used like a motif: "Between the stirrup and the ground, I mercy sought and mercy found." It is the same crucial fraction of a second, but where Greene's principal theme is (in words from *Brighton Rock*) "the appalling strangeness of the mercy of God," which makes for seconds in which one "murders and creates," in Lewis' world the fractions of seconds are much more ordinary and prosaic. Greene is interested in what leads up to that fraction of a second; Lewis is more interested in the consequences. Graham Greene's greatness lies in his dissection of the agony of an apparently great moral evil, that of murderers, whiskey-priests, adulterers, suicides; Lewis greatness lies in his dissection of the usual, the commonplace, the ordinary, the simple moment of courtesy or honesty or small-mindedness or thoughtlessness and the consequences of such moments.

Ransom's walk is through an unusually silent countryside: not only is this a hint, a reference to the title and a foreshadowing, it is as if Nature were holding its breath for a moment; things matter when even the smallest decisions are made. When he comes to the farmhouse, he finds a locked gate and a thick hedge. He throws his pack over the gate, and Lewis, as it were, pounces: "The moment he had done so, it seemed to him that he had not till now fully made up his mind—now that he must break into the garden if only to recover the pack. He became very angry with the

29

woman, and with himself, but he got down on his hands and knees and began to worm his way into the hedge'' (p. 10).

This passage illustrates one of the most remarkable, and most valuable, of Lewis' characteristics. The simple action (necessary to the action, but not for the character) has three important parts to it. First, although Ransom is still uncertain what he ought to do—''A nice fool he would look blundering in . . . with this silly story of a hysterical mother in tears because her idiot boy had been kept a half an hour late''—he feels, nonetheless, that ''he had committed himself to a troublesome duty on behalf of the old woman.'' His response to that perceived duty when it conflicts with his sense of how he will ''look,'' is simply to throw his pack over the hedge and thereby commit himself to action: there is something insouciant and trusting in his gesture, something of a leap in the dark; it is an act of trust in himself and in the cosmos. It is also, and rather oddly, the act of what we call an existentialist: Lewis might agree with Sartre that we are what we do, that we are the sum, not of our ideals or speculations or feelings, but of our actions. Morally and existentially, it is the action that matters.

Lewis always counseled his correspondents who wrote seeking religious advice that they should pay little attention to their feelings. To one, for example, Lewis wrote, ''Don't bother much about your feelings. When they are humble, loving, brave, give thanks for them; when they are conceited, selfish, cowardly, ask to have them altered. In neither case are they you, but only a thing that happens to you. What matters is your intentions and your behavior'' (*Letters*, p. 233). Actually, of course, the intentions matter to God; but to men, who cannot judge intentions, the actions matter. So that Ransom ''became very angry with the woman, and with himself'' is of little account: what matters is that—absurd as it is and absurd as he knows it to be—this forty-year-old professor ''got down on his hands and knees and began to worm his way through the hedge.''

The pattern is repeated constantly in Lewis' fiction. Indeed, it is repeated when a scratched and muddy Ransom gets through the thorns and nettles and sees that the farm ''was clearly the last place in the world where a stranger was likely to be asked to stay the night.'' But that does not matter—it is a mere ''feeling''— because Ransom has been bound ''by his unfortunate promise to the old woman.'' Ransom wants only a drink and a good night's sleep. But he hears something that sounds like a fight. He could leave. ''The last thing Ransom wanted was an adventure.'' But there it was before him: except by positively slinking away, he could not avoid it. Again, a self-image floats before him (like

Prufrock's seeing himself "descend the stair / With a bald spot in the middle of my hair"): when he sees two men fighting with a boy—the one he was obviously looking for, "he would like to have thundered out, 'What are you doing to that boy?' but the words that actually came—in a rather unimpressive voice—were, 'Here, I say! . . .'"

The style, like the emotion, does not really matter. The fact is that Ransom, in his shuffling way, simply did what had to be done. It emerges that Ransom knows one of the men, Devine (whose name suggests, surely, *corruptio optimi pessima*—i.e., the corruption of the best is the worst), an old schoolmate whom Ransom had particularly disliked—precisely because of a heavily ironic, life-denying and world-weary cynicism that Devine had developed as a schoolboy. Devine introduces his companion, a great physicist named Weston (whose name perhaps suggests the degeneration of the Western scientific tradition). In the brief dialogue which follows, Lewis quickly sketches the intellectual themes the novel will develop. Weston's gruff remark about "unscientific foolery," which shows his blinkered conviction that nothing but his science matters, anticipates by many years C. P. Snow's famous study of the gulf between the sciences and the humanities in *The Two Cultures*. Lewis, in this novel as well as the trilogy and, indeed, the rest of his work, will have much more to say about the evil effects of such a division. In general, Lewis adored distinctions and hated divisions. One quick touch—in Weston's threat to Harry: "in a properly governed country I'd know how to deal with you" (p. 14)—anticipates the totalitarian side of "Westonism." There is even a reference to vivisection, which Lewis occasionally attacks. And Ransom's experience simply contradicts "all the deep, irrational conviction of his age and class that such things could never cross the path of an ordinary person except in fiction." Indeed, the novel will develop a great deal about both rational and irrational fears and convictions.

There is a great deal in this first chapter, most of it springing from the typically Lewisian yoking of the homely—the ordinary and prosaic, in both the material and moral worlds—with the fantastic. This chapter, like nearly all the chapters in the whole of the trilogy, is fascinating in itself, unpretentiously pleasant at a first reading but yielding shrewdness, sense and eventually wisdom.

And so with the novel as a whole. Structurally, the novel is a good adventure story, following the conventional pattern of a thriller by H. G. Wells or Rider Haggard (a particular favorite of Lewis). A prelude gives us an ordinary situation which becomes, very quickly, extraordinary: Ransom finds himself kidnapped by

31

his academic colleagues and learns, on board a space ship, that he is being brought as a kind of human sacrifice for beings on some alien planet. The first climax of the novel occurs just after the trio lands on Malacandra (which only much later Ransom learns is Mars) as Ransom, armed only with a knife taken from a kitchen on the ship, flees. Ransom makes contact with some of the planet's natives, called *hrossa*, and befriends them so thoroughly that he is asked to join in their fight against their one natural enemy, a sea-monster known as a *hnakra*. After the fight, which is the second major climax, Ransom, following the orders of both the *hrossa* and other beings known as *eldila*, begins a long trip to a sacred place called Meldilorn where there is a splendid "trial" scene with the greatest of the *eldila*, called Oyarsa. This long climactic scene is concluded when Weston and Devine reappear and confront Oyarsa without showing they understand the reality of the experience at all. Oyarsa orders them all to return to earth, which they do, and then destroys the space ship. A Postscript introduces a narrator ("Lewis" himself) and ends with a brief "correspondence" between Ransom and "Lewis."

The obvious fact is that *Out of the Silent Planet* summarizes much less well than do most, even very good, science-fiction novels, probably because Lewis begins with a coherent philosophy and a fully worked out cosmology—it is the working out of that philosophy, especially the personal and inward part of it, in ways both subtle and obvious, against the great backdrop of the Christian cosmology that is the real achievement of the novel. (Most science-fiction novels are, by their nature, exploratory and philosophically tentative.)

In effect, what Lewis has done is to extend Christianity in both time and space. The extension in space is obvious enough: Christianity—as well as Ransom, Weston, and Devine—travels through the universe providing the basic ground—the values and sense of ultimate reality. All is ruled by God, of course—called Maledil, as Maledil the Young is the Son of God—but Lewis conceives each planet to have a kind of resident Spirit responsible for it: this is clearly an extension of the Christian legend of a personal Guardian Angel and the classical idea of a household god.

But Lewis was also interested in exploring the idea of time. Malacandra, as Lewis pictures it, is an extremely beautiful planet, but its beauty is the beauty of autumn, for Malacandra is coming to the end of its life. Since *Out of the Silent Planet* antedates the Second World War, we have some indication of the easily forgotten truth that it is not the Atom Bomb (alone) that makes men think that the End is near. If the novel lacks the sense of eschatological doom so characteristic of novels and films of the 1950s, it certainly shows that Lewis wanted to examine the idea of the End: he wanted to examine the near extinction of a world to examine the idea of purpose.

In general, the idea of "purpose"—that life has point, direction or some value beyond itself—must come from within or without. If within, then one subscribes, like George Bernard Shaw or even Arthur C. Clarke, to the idea that life is evolving itself into something greater—to the mystical affinities pictured in *Childhood's End* or simply to "brains," the more intelligent man Shaw imagined the "Superman" to be. If without, then of course one conceives of something superior to human life from which comes direction, purpose or value—a race of superior aliens, perhaps—if one assumes a series of ascending finite beings—or else, simply, God—if one accepts the infinite.

Lewis, obviously, takes the latter view. As Lewis imagines it, life consists of particular and finite manifestations of infinite life; a human life or the whole length of a planet's life is not destined to last forever; rather, the one flash of personal life (at least) is destined, at death, to be taken into life at an altogether different level—out of space and out of time entirely. It is the very existence of that level of life which gives point and purpose to human, indeed all temporal, life.

At its simplest the singular science of "Westonism" is a doomed and logically absurd attempt to hold on to one particular manifestation of life. It is logically absurd because there can be found within no particular value for preserving one manner of life, or one life, or any life. And it is doomed—though very dangerous—because, by definition, time destroys temporal life. The novel gives us a philosophical argument not merely by containing philosophic argument but, in its dramatic balance and design, by being a philosophic argument. "Things do not always happen as a man would expect," Lewis says mildly. "The moment of his arrival in an unknown world found Ransom wholly absorbed in a philosophical speculation" (p. 40). This is not so strange in a Lewis novel, but, in any case, what follows is not a discussion but Ransom's first sight of the new world—which is incomprehensible to him because he can see nothing but colors—"colours that refused to form themselves into things" (p. 42). This represents one of Lewis' most ingenious and subtlest strokes. First, of course, he gives us a Ransom who is a child in this new world, and Lewis communicates very well this sense of a child's awe and fear. But, second, when Ransom does begin to understand the meaning of things around him (like Adam, he must name things to comprehend them), he does so in this way: Ransom sees "strange upright shapes of whitish green," and behind them

33

something he can describe only as "the rose-coloured cloud-like mass." In a way that will become characteristic of him; Ransom struggles to understand the unknown in terms of the known—even in purely visual matters: "It looked like the top of a gigantic red cauliflower—and it was exquisitely beautiful in tint and shape" (p. 43).

This is ingenious and important because Weston, in contrast to Ransom, makes no attempt to *see* what is before him. Ransom's attempt may seem crude and childish—in the way that a child compares all things with the things in his home—but Ransom, in beginning with the known, comes far closer to understanding this new planet than does Weston. Weston is too sure of what is there: he wants mere real estate. He simply never really understands, because he refuses to see "the bright, still unintelligible landscape" (p. 44).

Despite the fact that Weston and Devine do not appear in the middle section of the novel—which Ransom has more or less to himself—the novel is really dialectical in design. Weston does not simply represent a modern version of the Mad Scientist, or Faust figure: his presence is always felt in the novel because his is an intellectual presence which, directly or indirectly, Ransom is always confronting.

Essentially, all the characters, but particularly Ransom and Weston, are dealing with fear. Fear is the given in this novel: the worlds are unknown, the inhabitants unimaginable, moral and ethical bearings uncertain: the characters' responses to this fear—or, rather, to the variety of fears that are distinguished with a connoisseur's fineness of analysis and nicety of judgment—constitute the substance and meaning of the novel. Devine, for example, responds to fear of the unknown by being a cynical materialist who is sure that what matters in life is power—power, money, domination, social position. He is Lewis' own finely etched version of Bunyan's Mr. Worldly Wiseman. It is clear that he is much more socially agreeable a person than Weston but a much worse man precisely because he lacks any of Weston's selfless-ness and mad idealism. But there is an interesting phrase Lewis uses to describe such a man. Ransom "felt for him that sort of distaste we feel for someone whom we have admired in boyhood for a very brief period and then outgrown." At school Devine was exactly the sort of boy who learned at once how to deal with a boy's fears: "Devine had learned just half a term earlier than any-one else that kind of humour which consists in a perpetual parody of the sentimental or idealistic cliches of one's elders." Even as an adult, Devine still makes his ironic references to "the white man's burden" and "the dear old school." But before he left Weden-

shaw Ransom had already begun to find L
Cambridge he had avoided him, wondering ʌ
one so flashy and, as it were, ready-made, cou
ful" (p. 15).

The key phrase is "ready-made." With Ransom
we are aware of some kind of development. With De   ʌere
is none: he is the sort of man who is simply the same ra ʌer cunning, success-driven being he was as a child. In his stasis, there is
no growth: Devine makes gestures; he never acts; and without
action, there is no morality. To a remarkable extent, all of Lewis'
novel deals with the (almost Browningesque) theme of the
development of the individual soul.

Ransom's soul is formed, so to speak, in little ways (to begin
with); Weston's is formed by the largest possible actions: a man
with a mad dream of colonizing space (madder, of course, in 1938
than it would appear in a post-Sputnik world) and who actually
does it. He acts. Devine goes along with him, but "He was quite
ready to laugh at Weston's solemn scientific idealism." Devine
certainly "didn't give a damn . . . for the future of the species or
the meeting of two worlds" (p. 30).

Neither Ransom nor Weston is "ready-made," however, because they share a love of knowledge. But Lewis, portrays Weston,
finally, as the man trapped by his own knowledge, by himself:
Ransom's professional knowledge of languages is not all that he
knows: there is some balance and proportion that makes it possible for him to see reality because he can really learn.

The wonderful scene in which Ransom first sees a *hross* is an
excellent, and key, example. Having already fled from the terrifying *sorns* and from the two humans who were trying to give him
to the *sorns* as a human sacrifice, Ransom is now trying to hide
from the approach of an alien who was "something like a penguin,
something like an otter, something like a seal; the slenderness
and flexibility of the body suggested a giant stoat" (p. 54).

Ransom assumes he will die: "He noted in a dry, objective
way that this was apparently to be the end of his story—caught
between a *sorn* from the land and a big, black animal from the
water." Then comes this paragraph:

> Then something happened which completely altered
> his state of mind. The creature, which was still steaming
> and shaking itself on the back and had obviously not
> seen him, opened its mouth and began to make noises.
> This in itself was not remarkable; but a lifetime of
> linguistic study assured Ransom almost at once that
> these were articulate noises. The creature was *talking*.

had a language. If you are yourself not a philologist, I am afraid you must take on trust the prodigious emotional consequences of this realization in Ransom's mind. A new world he had already seen—but a new, an extra-terrestrial, a non-human language was a different matter. Somehow he had not thought of this in connection with the *sorns*; now, it flashed upon him like a revelation. The love of knowledge is a kind of madness. In the fraction of a second which it took Ransom to decide that the creature was really talking, and while he still knew that he might be facing instant death, his imagination had leaped over every fear and hope and probability of his situation to follow the dazzling project of making a Malacandrian grammar. *An Introduction to the Malacandrian Language—The Lunar Verb—A Concise Martian-English Dictionary* . . . the titles flitted through his mind. And what might one not discover from the speech of a non-human race? The very form of language itself, the principle behind all possible languages, might fall into his hands. Unconsciously he raised himself on his elbow and stared at the black beast. It became silent. The huge bullet head swung round and lustrous amber eyes fixed him. There was no wind on the lake or in the wood. Minute after minute in utter silence the representatives of two so far-divided species stared each into the other's face (p. 55).

The more one considers this paragraph, the more interesting it becomes. In its key sentence, which is a clue to Lewis' whole approach as a writer—"The love of knowledge is a kind of madness"—one sees an unexpected distinction. Here the orderly, rational, conservative, the Apollonian self is not seen as the real source of knowledge at all: rather, Ransom raises his head from the protective earth and exposes himself to probable death to learn: the deep love of learning is really the Dionysian self, the more primitive side, wary but curious and willing to accept the disorder which attends all beginnings of knowledge. (Most adults find it difficult to learn new things, French or swimming or cooking, not because they dislike or fear the knowledge required or contained in those activities but because of the disarray, the messy disorder, the terrible fear of the unknown.)

Seen this way, Ransom's whole progress through the trilogy is really an entire life-as-learning cycle. Ransom had as little choice in going to Malacandra as does a baby being born. We learn about Ransom in school and see him almost refuse, in his innocence, in the evil-doing of Devine and Weston. But Ransom can really see: when he awakes on the space ship, and does not know what it is, he is struck by the beauty of the frosty night he sees from his window: "Pulsing with brightness as with some unbearable pain or pleasure, clustered in pathless and countless multitudes, dreamlike in clarity, blazing in perfect blackness, the stars seized all his attention, troubled him, excited him" (p. 21).

Ransom attends; he studies, he observes—even if he does not know at first what reality or the knowledge he is pursuing will bring him. Indeed, Ransom on the space ship was quivering with excitement: "he was poised on a sort of emotional watershed from which, he felt, he might at any moment pass into delirious terror or into an ecstasy of joy" (p. 23). Lewis the critic has written, "The first demand any work of art makes upon us is surrender. Look. Listen. Receive. Get yourself out of the way. There is no good asking first whether the work before you deserves such a surrender, for until you have surrendered you cannot possibly find out" (*An Experiment in Cricitism*, p. 19). Lewis, in his fiction, says that life itself makes a similar demand; moreover, he connects the learning—the discovery of what the reality is and what it means—with the emotional extremes of terror and joy.

So Ransom learns. He travels and to some extent learns to see himself and his home "as if for the first time." He is horrified to learn that the "moon" he thought he was watching was really the Earth. As always in Lewis, the learning is both inward and outward: Ransom sees space for the first time and "awe fell upon him" (p. 29), and yet when he fights with Devine and Weston, he does so "with a violence of which he would have believed himself incapable" (p. 20).

The theme of Ransom's physical courage reaches its climax in the fight with the sea-monster, the *hnakra*, when he fights valiantly. Early on, when Ransom thinks there is little or no chance of his returning to Earth alive, he considers death: "death could be faced, and rational fear of death could be mastered. It was only the irrational, the biological, horror of monsters that was the real difficulty" (p. 37). Even the fear has a consolation: "some fear, but more curiosity. It might mean death, but what a scaffold!" (p. 41). Curiosity is one of the best antidotes to fear, a real curiosity to see what is really out there. Ransom even distinguishes among *kinds* of fears: the *sorns* "appealed away from the Wellsian fantasies to an earlier, almost an infantile, complex of fears. Giants—ogres—ghosts—skeletons: these were its key words. Spooks on stilts, he said to himself; surrealistic bogy-men with their long faces." So Ransom makes nice distinctions among fears, and then—with his Apollonian and Dionysian sides making a kind of bargain—he decides that he will not commit suicide: more than that, "He felt a strange emotion of confidence and affection toward himself" (p. 47).

All Lewis' good characters come to a time when they like themselves: even in his religious writing, Lewis makes it clear that the path to God begins, not with some fake virtue like "living for others," but with a sense of pleasure and particularly a pleasure with and in oneself. The matter is clear in *The Screwtape Letters*: the devil Screwtape says clearly that all pleasure, as such, comes from God and is to be regarded—from the diabolical point of view—as extremely dangerous (p. 41). The "Patient" is lost to God because his tempter makes the mistake of allowing him two simple but very real pleasures—the reading of a good book and the taking of a good walk. Screwtape says, "The deepest likings and impulses of any man are the raw material, the starting-point, with which the Enemy [i.e., God] has furnished him" (p. 59). Screwtape advises young Wormwood to disguise the reality of pleasure from the human "by palming off vanity, bustle, irony, and expensive tedium as pleasures" (p. 58).

In other words, Lewis says that our search for God begins, very simply, with self-recognition and self-knowledge; we move to the plateau of pleasure that can lead us to Joy, at the very threshold of Heaven. In *The Great Divorce*, Lewis' magnificent dream-vision, the Guide, George MacDonald, says, "No soul that seriously and constantly desires joy will ever miss it" (p. 73). We begin with the Self and its pleasures and fears to go out from the Self (so to speak): because "every state of mind, left to itself, every shutting up of the creature within the dungeon of its own mind—is, in the end, Hell." And in contrast to the relativistic and subjective Hell Lewis imagines, there is Heaven (which Shaw, in *Man and Superman*, called the home of the masters of reality). "But Heaven is not a state of mind. Heaven is reality itself. All that is fully real is Heavenly" (p. 69).

In *The Great Divorce* we view life from the vantage point of the afterlife. In the Space Trilogy, although we view life as from a great distance and with a vast perspective, life is still seen as within time. However, Ransom pursued Reality by means of pleasure and Joy on the one hand and by avoiding and dealing with his fears on the other. The source of fear is invariably ignorance. Again, Lewis pictures a universe in which we understandably fear what we don't know but then are capable of either accepting or fighting the realities—but only if we have managed to get past the fears.

Ransom's love of knowledge, his "madness," is the first of his means of discovering the reality of Malacandra: and Lewis (in all his work) celebrates learning as if it were—as it sometimes is—love. After Ransom has established himself with the *hrossa*, "The wonder of it smote him most strongly when he found himself, about three weeks after his arrival, actually going for a walk. A few weeks later he had his favorite walks, and his favorite foods; he was beginning to develop habits" (p. 65). But at this stage there is a slight undercurrent of comedy caused by Ransom's half-conscious sense of intellectual superiority to the *hrossa*. But by knowing them, as individuals, as distinct personalities, he comes to realize the true situation: they are not more or less intelligent—the constant obsession of most space travelers—but different. In the differences Ransom learns: he learns about the *hrossa* and Malacandra and thus eventually comes to learn more about himself. After the slightly amusing first encounter, Ransom then has a profound discussion with his particular friend Hyoi who explains to him that *hrossa* have sex for only a brief period in their lives. Hyoi is puzzled that Ransom thinks this arrangement odd; he cannot understand why one would want to breed children, pleasurable though it is, at an inappropriate time in life. He does not understand *repetition*. "Would he want his dinner all day or want to sleep after he had slept? I do not understand." Ransom cannot satisfactorily explain the behavior of his own species. Hyoi says, "A pleasure is full grown only when it is remembered. You are speaking . . . as if the pleasure were one thing and the memory another. It is all one thing" (pp. 72-73).

There are two conclusions Ransom draws as he ponders this. The first is a rather predictable one: "Here, unless Hyoi was deceiving him, was a species naturally continent, naturally monogamous. And yet, was it so strange? Some animals he knew, had regular breeding seasons . . . . At last it dawned upon him it was not they, but his own species, that were the puzzle" (p. 74). But this self-recognition leads to more profound questioning: "What was the history of Man?"—a question that the rest of the trilogy tries to answer.

For the moment, Ransom simply hears the rather puzzled explanations from one of another species who obviously does not quite understand the (human) problem. Hyoi wonders, "how would we endure to live and let time pass if we were always crying for one day or one year to come back—if we did not know that every day in a life fills the whole life with expectation and memory and that these *are* that day?" (p. 74). Ransom (with the reader) of course reflects on the human attitude toward time—which is, usually, a refusal to accept the fact of

it. But Ransom, "unconsciously nettled on behalf of his own
world" (which, after all, "fell" in a sense that Malacandra never
did) points out that "Maleldil [God] has let in the *hnakra*," which
seems to suggest a failure of some kind. "Oh, but that is so different. I long to kill this *hnakra* as he also longs to kill me." Hyoi
despairs of making Ransom understand: 'How can I make you
understand, when you do not understand the poets''—poets who,
presumably, communicate the tragic grandeur of danger. "I do
not think the forest would be so bright, nor the water so warm,
nor love so sweet, if there were no danger in the lakes." He says,
"it is not a few deaths roving the world around him that make a
hnau [an unfallen being] miserable. It is a bent *hnau* that would
blacken the world" (pp. 74-75).

After this absorbing conversation, Ransom takes part in the
fight with the *hnakra*, a fight described with an almost Heming-
way-like sense of adventure and investiture of manhood. But at
the end of it, when Hyoi is shot by Weston or Devine, the grief-
stricken Ransom says, "it is through me that this has happened
. . . . I should have told you. We are all a bent race" (p. 81).

Seeing the truth again so clearly, Ransom must now set out on a
journey to Meldilorn to see Oyarsa. But he must also flee Weston
and Devine who are tracking him, and all the fears begin again:
he first must face the "hunted man's irrational instinct to give
himself up" (p. 85), as well as the "old terrestrial fears of some
alien, cold intelligence, super-human in power, sub-human in
cruelty" (p. 86). He copes with all these in part because of his
past experience. As he passes the purple forests he saw first in
Malacandra, he remembers his old fears for what they were—
nightmarish phantoms—which produced "a sort of sickness"
in him. So he has taken two steps backward: but progress is clearly possible. "Now, in the clear light of an accepted duty, he felt
fear indeed, but with it a sober sense of confidence in himself and
in the world, and even an element of pleasure" (pp. 86-87).
Of course, there are slips: when he first sees a *sorn* up close, he
feels fear, but again with an almost scholarly set of distinctions:
"the ideas of 'giant' and 'ghost' receded behind those of 'goblin'
and 'gawk' " (p. 92). But these fears nearly disappear as Ransom
indulges his "madness" of learning and actually learns from a
sorn the nature of Oyarsa and the other *eldila*—and can even en-
joy a kind of parody of a *hross*'s poem by a *sorn*. As he learns about
the *eldila* and their construction in light, which Lewis describes
in almost mystical terms (pp. 93-94), he suffers from his self-
recognition even as he rejoices in his new knowledge—in a process
of learning which almost fulfills Hyoi's sense of what a "day"
is, in which the anticipation, act and memory are all the same.

At Meldilorn, before the encounter with Oyarsa, Ransom's learning takes him to heights and depths, and everywhere he sees without and within. Lewis establishes a see-saw of emotion and perception: Ransom can feel awe of learning that Malacandra is a dying planet and be consoled beyond tragedy on hearing the simple truth "a world is not made to last forever, much less a race; that is not Maledil's way" (p. 100). And he can also know his own place "for the first time"—as when he picks out a planet in the sky and realizes with a shock it is the Earth, the Earth with the North Pole at the bottom, the Earth—"yes it was all there in that little disk—London, Athens, Jerusalem, Shakespeare"—and "it was the bleakest moment in all his travels" (p. 96). But he is also capable of feeling "the old lift of the heart, the soaring solemnity, the sense, at once sober and ecstatic, of life and power offered in unasked and unmeasured abundance" (p. 99).

The theme of self-recognition is most clear in the very sections in which Ransom is learning most about other things. He certainly sees history being made—which reinforces nicely Hyoi's insistence to him that the act and the memory are the same—as when he views the pictures (pp. 106-110) of the universe by Malacandrians: he is an Aeneas viewing the frescoes at Carthage, but he is more shocked than saddened when he sees himself in those pictures; but this was not nearly so bad as his seeing the arrival at Meldilorn of Devine and Weston and simply not recognizing them at all because "he, for one privileged moment, had seen the human form with almost Malacandrian eyes" (p. 125).

But self-recognition cannot be separated from what he learns about the universe: indeed, the whole point is that he understands himself more fully because he sees the relationship between the self and the rest of Reality more accurately. His learning is, as always, both very explicitly intellectual and emotional. Intellectually, he learns that he was brought to Malacandra because Oyarsa, the greatest of the Malacandrian *eldila*, had asked to speak to a human when Devine and Weston first came to his planet. Ransom again learns the power of fear, and he must explain to Oyarsa why Devine and Weston did not honorably deal with him—because "bent creatures," he says, "are full of fears" (p. 122). He learns that the Malacandrians have called the Earth the "silent planet" because ever since the fall of Earth's Oyarsa (i.e., Satan) the Earth has been sealed off from the rest of the universe. Ransom learns much from Oyarsa: he learns that there are three kinds of *hnau* (rational, material beings) on Malacandra: the *hrossa*, whom Ransom knows well, the poets and hunters and adventurers; the *pfifltriggi* who (like Wagner's—and Arthur Rackham's—Nibelungs) live under the earth and make artifacts;

and the *seroni*, *sorns*, who are the thinkers, the analytical philosophers.

But Ransom does not merely learn the facts about Malacandra; he also learns some of the implications of those facts. As the *sorn* Augray remarks to Ransom, "Your thought must be at the mercy of your blood . . . or you cannot compare it with thought that floats on a different blood" (p. 103). Everything about what Ransom learns has the effect of leading Ransom (and the reader) out from the limitations of his (silent) planet, even his species.

Ransom's learning is capped by his hearing the funeral song which the *hrossa* sing. Although Lewis gives an excellent prose poem as the song, it is the paragraph before it which contains the wonder of this art and new way of feeling that is opened to Ransom:

> To every man, in his acquaintance with a new art, there comes a moment when that which before was meaningless first lifts, as it were, one corner of the curtain that hides its mystery, and reveals, in a burst of delight which later and fuller understanding can hardly ever equal, one glimpse of the indefinite possibilities within. For Ransom, this moment had now come in his understanding of Malacandrian song. Now first he saw that its rhythms were based on a different blood from ours, on a heart that beat more quickly, and a fiercer internal heat. Through his knowledge of the creatures and his love for them he began, ever so little, to hear it with their ears. A sense of great masses moving at visionary speeds, of giants dancing, of eternal sorrows eternally consoled, of he knew not what and yet what he had always known, awoke in him with the very first bars of the deep-mouthed dirge, and bowed down his spirit as if the gate of heaven had opened before him (p. 131).

By means of his courage in overcoming his fears of the unknown (as well as the strange, the alien, the weird-looking) and by means of his intelligence, but most of all by his love, Ransom has experienced entirely new emotions, which, when felt, he realized he had always known: through love, he discovers the chords we can all hear, the bonds we all feel.

In splendid, and at times comic, contrast to Ransom's progress to wisdom is the spectacle of the interview between Oyarsa and Weston. Devine's cynicism is exposed most hollowly when, after the heaven-moving dirge of the *hrossa* and Oyarsa "unbodies" the corpses, Devine can only mutter, "That would be a trick worth knowing on Earth . . . . Solves the murderer's problem about the disposal of the body, eh?" (p. 132). But Devine, the "ready-made," hardly even matters any more morally: as Oyarsa says of him, he is nothing "but greed." "He is now only a talking animal" (p. 139).

However, Weston is "only bent." The dialectical structure of the novel is clear when Oyarsa and Weston talk because the real conflict is a philosophical one; Ransom has learned enough to be, in fact, the translator for Oyarsa and Weston. In a central scene, Weston explains his dream of colonizing space for Earthlings. Lewis' translator device is excellently calculated to show the meaninglessness of much of "Westonism." For example, Weston says, "Life is greater than any system of morality; her claims are absolute." Ransom's "translation" is as follows:

> He says . . . that living creatures are stronger than the question whether an act is good or bent—no, that cannot be right—he says it is better to be alive and bent than to be dead—no—he says—I cannot say what he says, Oyarsa, in your language. But he does go on to say that the only good think is that there should be very many creatures alive (p. 136).

Oyarsa is astounded by this because Weston tried to kill Ransom. He says to Weston, "Any kind of creature will please you if only it is begotten by your kind as they now are. It seems to me, Thick One, that what you really love is no completed creature but the very seed itself: for that is all that is left" (p. 138).

Weston suffers from a delusion that he is talking to a kind of primitive witch doctor. (He tried enticing the Malacandrians with colored beads!) He denounces what he calls Oyarsa's "defeatist trash" and rejects the life-death cycle that time means. "You say your Maleldil let all go dead. Other one, Bent One, he fight, jump, live—not all talkee-talkee. Me no care Maleldil. Like Bent One better: me on his side" (p. 140).

What at first appears to be only a joke proves to be, in *Perelandra*, much more.

V

PERELANDRA—THEME AND POEM OF MAN

Lewis began writing another science-fiction novel, *The Dark Tower*, almost immediately after he had finished *Out of the Silent Planet*. He kept the narrative device of using himself as a kind of character, an important medieval touch: not many authors since Chaucer have entered their own works. And he retained Ransom as well as the academic setting of Cambridge. The novel has on its first page an enticing remark about "how thin is the crust which protects 'real life' from the fantastic" (*The Dark Tower*, p.17). It introduces a Scottish rationalist named MacPhee (who will figure in *That Hideous Strength*) as one of the many thoughtful characters who discuss the nature of time. There are some provocative references to J.W.N. Dunne's *An Experiment with Time*, and the theories of time are dramatized by an invention of a "chronoscope": by it, the characters can see into another time, although they have no idea what time—past or future—they are watching. The plot develops as one of the young Cambridge dons sees his double and his fiancee; he somehow crosses into the other time zone, and when he does his double becomes lost in "our" time. The young don lost in other time reads treatises on time and learns that there are dimensions of time, whole modes of reality, of which we know nothing. In one of the treatises, he reads this sentence: "In the year 60, Z, who had come to chronology from the study of folklore, propounded the theory that certain fabulous creatures, and other images which constantly appeared in the myths of widely separated peoples and in dreams, might be glimpses of realities which exist in a time closely adjacent to our own" (p. 88). After another page or so, Lewis' manuscript breaks off in mid-sentence.

Lewis never finished this extremely interesting and promising novel; it was published as a fragment in 1977, given the title *The Dark Tower* by its editor, Walter Hooper. Lewis wrote no fiction for almost five years, years in which he grew powerfully as a writer, creating the first of his religious books, two of his characteristically concise critical works, and what has proved to be his most popular book, *The Screwtape Letters*.

But why did he abandon this second novel? Two possibilities are these: he came to write the sentence about myths and dreams existing quite actually in another dimension and (almost at once) realized that *that* was the theme he wanted to explore, and he had begun a novel that did not really allow the dramatic or narrative development of that idea. (We often say that a writer must write his book and then discover what it is about: here is a graphic example.) Second, the story he had begun was exciting and interesting, but it did not permit any moral significance: it was, perhaps, too purely philosophical, too abstract, too far from the moral centers of reality for Lewis.

Certainly the great novel he did write, *Perelandra*, develops the theme of myth and history in a singularly gorgeous book that reads like a long prose poem: the romantic Lewis, the writer who burned with an unashamedly Shelleyan intensity, is nowhere more ecstatically himself than in *Perelandra*. Certainly the increase in assured mastery from *Out of the Silent Planet* to *Perelandra* is like the achieving of authorial selfhood on Lewis' part; and, indeed, this achieving of the Self is what *Perelandra* is all about.

Precisely because it is the richer, more cogently organized, and more brilliantly argued book, *Perelandra* is more easily discussed and described than *Out of the Silent Planet*. Even the summary in *Perelandra* of *Out of the Silent Planet* is excellent (pp. 81-82). But it is more than a summary of Weston's "idea that humanity, having now sufficiently corrupted the planet where it arose, must at all costs contrive to seed itself over a larger area" (p. 81). We realize that we are reading a different kind of novel when Lewis drives in this point about Westonism: "But beyond this lies the sweet poison of the false infinite—the wild dream that planet after planet, system after system, in the end galaxy after galaxy, can be forced to sustain, everywhere and forever, the sort of life which is contained in the loins of our own species—a dream begotten by the hatred of death upon the fear of true immortality . . . " (pp. 81-81).

The end of the sentence contains the key words for *Perelandra*— dreams, hatred, fear, death and immortality. For *Perelandra* asks questions about life that are arranged like ever-narrowing concentric philosophic circles, and the inmost question is this:

Is life finally a thing of horror or of joy? It is the kind of question that can be best asked in Lewis' combination of fantasy and science fiction with a dose of diabolic Gothicism: the Gothic element is strong (if not immediately obvious) because the premise of this philosophic voyage is fear, the starting point, the original, the basic human condition; and later in the novel Ransom's supreme, and supremely terrifying, temptation is the surrender to the idea that life is full of horror. It was early in *Out of the Silent Planet* that Ransom felt himself "poised on a sort of emotional watershed from which, he felt, he might at any moment pass into delirious terror or into an ecstasy of joy" (p. 23). But it is in *Perelandra* that we track Ransom into both a physical and philosophic terror and joy.

Almost literally tracking Ransom is what terrifies the narrator ("Lewis"): "I realised now that my emotion was neither more, nor less, nor other, than Fear" (p. 10). And he is afraid of two things—one, of meeting an *eldil* (thus suggesting that the universe is vast, strange, peculiar and, simply, not what it appears to be); two, of becoming "drawn in" (that is, afraid of being taken out of himself, away from the comfortably familiar security of his own home, his values, his philosophic base). The Absurdist, almost Existential, sense of dislocation, of alienation, is the important premise on which the novel is based: "How if food itself turns out to be the very thing you can't eat, and home the very place you can't live, and your very comforter the person who makes you uncomfortable?" (p. 19). The narrator represents us in his fears of the unknown. Because of the real *eldila*, or angels, the narrator is afraid of spectres; moreover, when he is convinced the spectre is illusory, the illusion "simply adds the further terror of madness itself—and then on top of that the horrible surmise that those whom the rest call mad have, all along, been the only people who see the world as it really is" (p. 14). When the narrator doubts his sanity, he wonders if sanity itself had ever been "more than a convention—a comfortable set of blinkers, an agreed mode of wishful thinking, which excluded from our view the full strangeness and malevolence of the universe we are compelled to inhabit?" (p. 15).

The novel, in other words, begins by making us ask whether the universe might be even more horrible than it appears to be. We are frightened and homeless creatures, longing for reason and sanity, tormented by fears, forever searching for home, for a base, for reality.

Out of the Silent Planet develops the theme of the passionate desire for learning, and *Perelandra* takes that theme to the edge of the intelligible and the bearable. Old longings, half-remembered dreams, history, myths, legends, physical needs, questioning and questing—all these are the means by which Ransom learns what Reality is and how the individual achieves, and can lose, a Self—his soul or identity.

Because of his Malacandrian adventures, Ransom is sent to Perelandra, or Venus, by the *eldila*. On Perelandra, he finds an innocent world, sinless and Edenic. Sin is about to enter into it, and Ransom must save this Eden from the misery that the Fall of the "Bent One" has, in corrupting our Adam and Eve, produced in our world.

Of course, Ransom, when he lands on Perelandra, feels some fear and homelessness, which Lewis has so carefully established as the background—or as the question which the novel will try to answer. But the principal physical feature of Perelandra is a perfect means for Lewis to explore this theme: Ransom finds himself on an island which floats, like a huge rubber raft but with fantastically gorgeous vegetation, over the equally gorgeous Perelandrian seas. The seas are at times calm, at times stormy; the islands float together, break apart, come together again but with no apparent pattern: it seems to be all chance; sometimes the islands whip dangerously on storm-tossed seas; sometimes the islands are pleasure lands with visual splendors and physical sensations that seem almost drug-induced because they are described with the startling and fantastic, almost disturbing, suddenness and vividness of a dream: surely, some of Lewis' most gorgeous, golden paragraphs are in this, his most physically beautiful, novel.

In this novel, there are visual needs as great as the need for food. Ransom learns that he has been homesick for his own world when, after a time, he comes to the Fixed Lands, and his "eyes, long accustomed to the medley of curves and contours in the floating islands, rested on the pure lines and stable masses of this place with great refreshment" (p. 80). Later, when Ransom is underground, he "found himself thinking about light as a hungry man thinks about food" (p. 176). But taste generally is important in a characteristically Lewisian way: "It is to be noted all through this story that while Ransom was on Perelandra his sense of taste had become something more than it was on Earth: it gave knowledge as well as pleasure, though not a knowledge that can be reduced to words" (p. 162). The knowledge is very important—and what it "means" (though it is as hard to describe as music) becomes clear by the end of the novel. Ransom learns about Pleasure.

In his characteristically dialectical and contentious way, Lewis opposes Fear and Pleasure in *Perelandra*: certainly, Ransom experiences both in his adventure. When he first sees the Green Woman, the Eve of Perelandra, he experiences Fear in the form of a terror of hallucinations (p. 54). Fears of this kind escalate to the climactic scenes of his battles with "Weston" over the Green Woman; in facing Satan, he faces evil; and in facing evil he faces extremes of terror—a physical fear of death and the horror of despair (pp. 161-171).

These fears are overcome by battle—a literal battle, as bloody as Siegfried's fight with Fafner—and by his learning even through taste. Early on Perelandra, Ransom tastes a yellow fruit: "It was like the discovery of a totally new *genus* of pleasures, something unheard of among men, out of all reckoning, beyond all covenant. For one draught of this on Earth wars would be fought and nations betrayed" (p. 42). Before that fruit, Ransom had a drink which gave him "a quite astonishing pleasure" which was "almost like meeting Pleasure itself for the first time" (p. 35). Even the sense of smell is involved: "his contact with soil and bush appeared to wake new odours that darted into his brain and there begot wild and enormous pleasures" (p. 190).

The Fear and the Pleasure, which Lewis pictures with an almost Platonic kind of isolating purity, are not only opposed in themselves but have opposing tendencies: Fear is a phantom and Pleasure is actual. Fear leads to despair, a refusal to live or see any longer. Pleasure leads to Joy, and ultimately to God Who is Reality itself.

Much of the novel takes place, so to speak, on one or the other of these two tracks—the Fear-Despair track or the Pleasure-Joy track. The link between these two tracks is Lewis' sense of battle—Ransom must do moral and physical battle with a Devil who has possessed Weston's body (the Devil cannot get to Perelandra without human cooperation, but Weston's self, or soul, is then consumed by the Devil). Related to this battle theme are the ordering principles of opposites and hierarchy. Ransom accepts as easily, it being part of the natural order, his role of commoner to the Green Woman's Queen (p. 67) as she accepts her place in relation to the *eldila* (pp. 82-83): the Great Chain of Being is secure on Perelandra. Similarly, Ransom moves from seeing the fusion of opposites in the Green Woman's face—she is both Pagan goddess and Madonna (p. 64)—to understanding the "fundamental polarity which divides all created things" at the end of the novel (p. 200). The polarity is the means of achieving separation, and thus identity, and at the same time a connection with the rest of reality. Ransom learns about this reality not only from his tastes and pleasures as well as his physical and aesthetic (especially visual) needs but also from dreams, myths, and even music:

music reveals to him the presence of other beings (the eldila) and thus other modes of Reality; indeed, Lewis seems to illuminate Keats' famous line, "Heard melodies are sweet, but those unheard / Are sweeter," when he describes the "phantom sense of vast choral music" surrounding Ransom (p. 66).

But Lewis pinpoints a source of Fear in the very pleasures (from food to music) that Ransom can use as a mode of knowledge. After Ransom eats the incredible yellow fruit, he thinks it would be a "vulgarity" to want to repeat so fine a pleasure (p. 43). But Ransom considers this later and realizes there is more to it: "This itch to have things over again . . . was it possibly the root of all evil? No: of course the love of money was called that. But money itself—perhaps one valued it chiefly as a defense against chance, a security for being able to have things over again . . ." (p. 48). Ransom learns that this need for Repetition is one of the marks of Fallen Man: the Green Woman cannot understand his desire to repeat experiences, and the Devil tries to teach her what it means to "keep" things (p. 138). From the Green Woman, he learns to see Reality as a series of waves (since we live in time), not one of which can ever come back or be brought back. But there is no need to—so long as one trusts and does not fear— because, in a key line of hers, "The fruit we are eating is always the best fruit of all" (p. 83). Ransom spends much of the novel absorbing the truth of this saying. (It is worth recalling that Screwtape had advised Wormwood to keep the Patient away, at all costs, from the Present—to keep him brooding about the Past or dithering about the Future.)

Thus, "Westonism" is a refusal to accept Reality, a refusal to see that life is a series of waves, that everything is always different, that God (or Maleldil) never repeats anything.

Closely related to this theme of Repetition is the other illusory protection money gives—a protection from chance. Philosophically, the principal theme of the novel is the problem of destiny and free will. Ransom suffers from much less loneliness on Perelandra than he had on Malacandra because he had thought that "mere chance" had taken him there. But on Perelandra, "he knew that he was part of a plan" (p. 50). The magnificent conclusion of the novel is devoted to the almost mystical resolution of this problem. Ransom knows deeply from his own actions (and he retains the wound in his heel, bleeding always, as a result of his fight with the Weston-Devil) that choice is possible; he learns that the meaning of that choice is vaster than he had supposed. "All that is made seems planless to the darkened mind, because there are more plans than it looked for." From the eldila, he also learns that "There seems no plan because it is all plan: there seems no centre because it is all centre'' (p. 218). In a moment of mystical revelation beyond words, Ransom "thought he saw the Great Dance," which is Reality itself, and when he looked and tried to follow the skeins and patterns, he saw "at the very zenith of complexity, complexity was eaten up and faded, as a thin white cloud fades into the hard blue burning of the sky, and a simplicity beyond all comprehension, ancient and young as spring, illimitable, pellucid, drew him with cords of infinite desire into its own stillness" (pp. 218-19).

But Lewis is not content to suggest that Ransom simply absorbs, by mystical intuition, unexpressible truths about the destiny and free will and the order of the universe (though he does): Ransom must do battle, and it is a grimly physical battle, like the battle of the single champions in an epic. But that physical battle—which makes for an entertainingly exciting climax—merely represents the philosophical differences, first between the real Weston but later between the philosophy of Ransom and the evil nihilism of the Devil.

Weston had already given himself to the Devil at the end of *Out of the Silent Planet* because he valued the force which the Devil represents: Maleldil, he complained, is all "talkee-talkee" (p. 140). Weston had, in fact, become a convert to what he calls "biological philosophy" and develops a vague religion that is clearly like the Creative Evolution of Henri Bergson and Bernard Shaw: he believes in the "Life-Force." After Weston and Ransom argue about this and related matters, with Ransom wondering where in this Force value is to be located, Weston's takeover by the Devil becomes the more complete as, ironically, Weston comes more and more to worship "*Pure* spirit: the final vortex of self-thinking, self-originating activity" (p. 92). (But perhaps that is not so ironic: naturally, the Devil would want humans to worship spirit and would even cultivate the very word "spiritual.")

But when the temptation of the Green Woman begins, there is little real debate: the Devil merely uses words; he is not interested in ideas or debate (as Goethe and Shaw imagine him to be); he wants only to consume, totally and forever, other beings. He tempts Eve first merely to think about what God has forbidden her—to sleep on the Fixed Lands, which suggests that the desire to stay on the Fixed Lands is a refusal to accept the flux of life, represented by the Floating Islands. The Devil asks Eve why God should insist that the King and Queen be separated for now, and he conceals from her the truth that they must be separate for a time to achieve identity or Selfhood before they meet and marry and begin to complete human life on Perelandra. The Devil tempts her to become like the gods and thus to become what he calls "a full woman" (p. 105).

Ransom is, after this first encounter, "conscious of a sense of triumph" (p. 107). But, although he knows clearly that a great calamity has been averted and, indeed, feels intensely the "unheard" music, it was only a battle, not the war. The second encounter is a series of debates between the Devil and Ransom as the Green Woman listens fitfully. They begin when Ransom finds a horribly mutilated frog; this is an "intolerable obscenity" in a world without evil: "It would have been better, or so he thought at that moment, for the whole universe never to have existed than for this one thing to have happened" (p. 109). The moral urgency of the question of evil still throbs for the man who had already written *The Problem of Pain*. Ransom finds a trail of dead frogs and sees "Weston" killing them: he glimpses the imbecilic nature of evil; its craziness and idiotic pointlessness are the moral equivalents of the most intense physical pain.

The fascinating account of a second Fall, just averted, is based on the assumption that evil is a perversion of good and that great evil is a hairsbreadth perversion of great good. The key concept remains the "wave," and the Devil insists that Ransom wants the Green Woman to remain fixed in the past. He tells her boldly that he offers her "Death in abundance"; for that, therefore she must be courageous. The Devil suggests that God really wants to be disobeyed—though the Green Woman does not know how she could "step out of His will" (pp. 114-16). But the Devil goes on with very powerful, almost right, very Romantic arguments: he tells her stories about brave, misunderstood women who face their isolation (caused invariably by their desire for power and assertion of the self) with noble tragedy. Ransom reacts with a shock when he sees the first human look on the woman's face—a look of a "very *good* tragedy queen" (p. 127). Of course, tragedy is a noble response to pain and evil; but the Devil's temptation is the strange appeal to heroic behavior as pure posture, to convalesce beautifully in a hospital before one is ill.

Through all this, Ransom is tempted to despair. Perhaps the Devil is right; Ransom is a mere mortal man. The Devil is a great spirit who lives from century to century. Perhaps he thinks the (explicitly named) "Creative Evolution" *is* "the deepest truth" (p. 121). There is almost a temptation to surrender to horror itself when Ransom perceives that the old real Weston is being consumed: "he had pictured the lost souls as being still human; now, as the frightful abyss which parts ghosthood from manhood yawned before him, pity was almost swallowed up in horror—in the unconquerable revulsion of the life within him from positive and self-consuming Death" (p. 130). Now it is clear: there is no longer Weston, but an "Un-man," and the appeal to Death is based on a terrible, overwhelming fear of life, of the Reality God creates.

The Devil's, or Un-man's, appeal to the Unselfish Woman (always the negative form of a positive virtue) is almost successful: Ransom finds the Green Woman dressed in bird feathers, and he realizes where the Un-man got the feathers—through more pain and death. For one moment she is sexually attractive to Ransom (as opposed to the rest of their time together, when they are so different that Ransom could no more be sexually attracted to her than he would be to even the most gorgeous petunia). She looks in a mirror and learns what fear is: like Siegfried, she begins with innocence and must learn fear; the rest of us begin with fear and must glimpse innocence—reconstruct it, so to speak. She learns what *keeping* is—as she becomes prey to the desire for Repetition which Ransom had explored earlier. But the *imago* the Devil had been offering the Green Woman was not chiefly concerned with vanity. "The image of her beautiful body had been offered to her only as a means to awake the far more perilous image of her great soul. The external and, as it were, dramatic conception of the self was the enemy's true aim. He was making her mind a theatre in which that phantom self should hold the stage. He had already written the play" (pp. 138-39).

The pursuit of the phantom self is precisely what sets Ransom off in his quest for the Real. What matters? First, "The fate of a world really depended on how they behaved in the next few hours." And more: "Either something or nothing must depend on individual choices. And if something, who could set bounds to it?" (p. 142). Third, Ransom's name is important (Lewis having forgotten or simply ignoring the fact that "Ransom" was not, in *Out of the Silent Planet*, supposed to be his real name): there are no accidents, and Ransom stands as the man now who must pay the debt that must be paid for the preservation (as Jesus had paid for the redemption) of the good. At last, knowing that he must really fight the Devil, he is aware that he must "enact what philosophy only thinks" (p. 148). He comes to two conclusions: one is that he must fight; the other is that "Predestination and freedom were apparently identical" (p. 149).

And so, epic fashion, the great battle begins. Ransom shouts an Anglo-Saxon line from *The Battle of Maldon* and "His hands taught him terrible things," while he learns what hatred is really for, a real, not a phantom, help in a just battle. But battles are not easily won. In a lull, the exhausted warriors talk after Ransom has felt that "mere bigness and loneliness overbore him" (p. 165). Ransom tries to tell the real Weston (who appears for a moment in his own body) that death is not so important after all. But then Weston, consumed now by the Devil, assaults Ransom with many of our own twentieth-century moral assumptions. Like Camus' Stranger, the Devil says it is important "to live as long as you can" (p. 167). He says, "the good things are now—a thin little rind of what we call life, put on for show, and then—the *real* universe for ever and ever" (p. 168). He claims, "reality is neither rational nor consistent nor anything else . . . . The only point in anything is that there isn't any point" (p. 169). He goes on through Spiritualism (arguing that accounts of the dead are always horrific) and several other modernisms before Ransom feels horror: "Horror of death such as he had never known, horror of the terrified creature at his side, descended upon Ransom: finally, horror with no definite object" (p. 171).

It takes a long time to kill the Devil. Ransom does so only after he has seen Weston's Self being lost entirely, Weston's small self being "melted down" into Satan. The Devil's last assault is intellectual: Ransom is made to believe "that he had been living all his life in a world of illusion." He thinks that "Reality lived— the meaningless, the un-made, the omnipotent idiocy to which all spirits were irrelevant and before which all efforts were vain" (p. 180) He orders these thoughts out of his brain and at last destroys Weston's body. The great fight ends with Ransom's recalling that he had once seen an ugly insect which, on closer inspection, proved to be a lovely leaf. There is a thin line between beauty and ugliness, reason and madness, bravery and cowardice, right and wrong: but the thinness of the line does not mean that it is not there, that it is unreal.

Thus, Ransom is now ready for the great finale wherein so much is revealed to him. As we have seen, Lewis' oddly rational mysticism pictures Reality as "The Great Dance" in which all is plan and pattern, order and beauty. But Ransom learns something more, a statement of what suddenly proves to be the most important theme in the novel. The Adamite King tells Ransom that "All is gift," and that "The best fruits are plucked for each by some hand that is not his own." We find the Self, we find Reality most surely when we are plucking fruit for others—as Ransom had to preserve the innocence of a whole planet not his own—and can express joy and gratitude when someone else brings fruit for us. The King says that there is no Fixed Land: "Always one must throw oneself into the wave," and one recalls that the same wave never comes again. One must beware of "cold love and feeble trust" and see that Reality must be accepted and the Self must be achieved—though invariably in unexpected way (pp. 208-10).

Perelandra is Lewis' most poetic, most ecstatic novel. In it, he offers a powerfully coherent view of life that is based on the premise that we are free to see, think and choose. Hamlet says that "There's nothing either good nor bad but thinking makes it so." Similarly, Ransom says to the Devil that the "account a man gives of the universe . . . depends very much on where he is standing." To which the Devil replies that the place we choose to stand is the outside where things have an illusion of beauty, like a beautiful body or Perelandra itself. "All the colours and pleasant shapes are merely where it ends, where it ceases to be. Inside, what do you get? Darkness, worms, heat, pressure, salt, suffocation, stink" (p. 169). We learn from the Devil that the universe does in truth contain horrors, but to insist that horror is the *ultimate* reality is to refuse to see, as Ransom did in his rooms at Cambridge, the ugly insect turn into a beautiful leaf, to refuse to see that the ultimate reality is the joy and splendor achieved after one has gone through and coped with the slime and horror. Life is a call to battle and through it a call to joy: the moral part of the battle is the fight with the slime, horror, and phantom fears.

Having traveled to two planets and having seen their spirits Ares and Aphrodite, having seen how everything can offer light and meaning, from the merest scrap of a legend to a whole philosophy, having seen what a terrible battle the search for identity and reality can be, the reader of C. S. Lewis is now ready for Lewis' view of the strangest planet of all. As he returns to Earth, the reader, like Ransom, will probably need the wishes offered in the noble farewell from Perelandra—which is much more moving than *Star War*'s famous wish for mere "force"—"The splendour, the love, and the strength be upon you" (p. 222).

It is clear then: Lewis says that life is for learning and that life is a call to battle and a call to joy: but without a knowledge of Perelandra, Venus, the goddess of love, the call becomes grotesquely distorted—into mere force, a hideous strength.

VI

HOW STRENGTH GROWS HIDEOUS

Perelandra is the kind of novel one reads slowly and savors lovingly. The very landscape, as well as the Miltonic exchanges between the characters, encourages slow, reflective reading. The contrast with the next novel in the Space Trilogy could hardly be more startling: more than one reader has confessed to an all-night first reading of *That Hideous Strength*, which, in contrast to the *longueurs* of *Perelandra*, has the crisp tautness of a first-rate detective or adventure story. There are really only three major characters (actually, personifications of ideas rather than characters) in *Perelandra*. In *That Hideous Strength*, we find a dozen cunningly sculpted characters. In the first two novels of the trilogy, the plot develops along a straight line, following the adventures—and the point of view—of Ransom; there are two parallel plots in *That Hideous Strength*, with multiple points of view.

But the greatest difference lies in the relationship between the novel and the time in which it was written. While *Out of the Silent Planet* could be "dated" by the scientific state of the art of moon travel and by the twentieth-century concern with the possibility of space travel and colonization, *Perelandra* is as timeless as *Paradise Lost*. But *That Hideous Strength* is a specifically, intentionally modern novel: it is about the modern condition; it is addressed very specifically to a modern audience, aware, Lewis hopes, of the specifically modern problems with which the novel is concerned. It is the only one of Lewis' novels that could be called "modern" in these senses: it is of and for its time.

And yet, in its design, purpose and technique, it might almost be called a very medievally modern novel. How rare for Lewis to use "modern" in his title: the subtitle of the novel is "A Modern

Fairy-Tale for Grown-Ups." He had in mind the medieval fairy tale with its "cottages, castles, woodcutters, and petty kings," and he wrote an up-dated version of the fairy tale with such relish that the whole novel is suffused with the sheer *fun* of the form itself. Most obviously, Lewis imitates the medieval writers in setting out, with a craftsman's delight, to use an already existing literary form both for a special purpose and for the more general purpose of producing a good example of that form—as, say, Chaucer filled *The Canterbury Tales* with examples of what can be done with given forms, how stately a romance can be, how funny a *fabliau* can be—like a Beethoven showing what splendid things can be done with a waltz or a fugue. There is a kind of delighted—and extremely rare—*virtuosity* in Lewis' creation of this "modern fairy-tale for grown-ups"; it is the kind of thing a craftsman (as opposed to the more modern, more Romantic artist) takes delight in doing—a demonstration of the craftsman's skill but at the same time a humble, almost selfless demonstration of the possibilities of the form itself. Whoever would have thought of using a fairy tale for the serious purpose Lewis has in mind? Whoever would have thought of adding to the joke by naming a lesbian character Fairy Hardcastle?

The issues in *That Hideous Strength* are so serious that it is hard to remember—especially in analysis—that these issues are treated in a novel that is such a delightful *jeu d'esprit*. There is a grace and lightness about *That Hideous Strength* that makes it unique in Lewis' adult fiction and unique in novels with serious theses. It would be as if a comic gem like *The Importance of Being Earnest* also contained a moving analysis of the declining greatness of the British Empire. Or suppose a great thesis novel like *Sybil* rippled throughout with the occasional high style, wit and elegance of some of Disraeli's sentences. It is very hard to think of any novel, past or present, that has quite this (again, almost medieval) combination of gravity and gaiety: perhaps it shows there is still life in the sound classical and medieval prescription that art should both delight and instruct.

Unfortunately, in analysis, it is much easier to discuss, and thus distort in emphasis, the serious side, the thesis. "This," Lewis tells us, "is a 'tall story' about devilry, though it has behind it a serious 'point' which I have tried to make in my *Abolition of Man*" (p. 7).

This brilliant and pithy book is central to an understanding of Lewis generally—as well as *That Hideous Strength* in particular. *The Abolition of Man* is also a classic statement of modern Christian humanism (though Lewis would probably have disliked the term)—whether one takes that to mean the kind of humanism a

Christian might lay claim to or the kind of humanism that a non-Christian derives from Christianity and the Christian tradition. Lewis presents a definition of "man" and then proceeds to show that, how, and with what results this conception of man is being abolished in the modern world. This little book, as brilliantly reasoned and written as any of his books, is, however, page for page, one of the *heaviest* of his books: Lewis takes care that his reader understand that he is trying to represent "man" as he has been understood in the Western and Eastern worlds for five thousand years.

Lewis argues that "man" has conceptually degenerated into a creature who grunts about his feelings and little else. He cites an example from a textbook (and the examples could, if anything, be even more easily found today) in which the authors argue that a man who says, "This waterfall is sublime," was "not making a remark about the waterfall, but a remark about his own feelings." The authors—attacked so vigorously by Lewis that they are given the concealing names of Gaius and Titius—speaking for many in the modern world, go on to say, "We appear to be saying something very important about something: and actually we are only saying something about our own feelings" (*The Abolition of Man*, p. 14). The same message is with us, going even deeper, even less examined or criticized, today: a poem means whatever you want it to mean, you have to trust your feelings, and you have to take care of yourself (alone).

Gaius and Titius devote nearly all their time to the debunking of sentimental cliches, and Lewis argues that the debunking is not of bad emotion but of emotion—precisely because Gaius and Titius argue that an expression of emotion has merely to do with oneself, not with an objective reality. Lewis has two objections. First, he says that most young people do not have to be guarded from "a weak excess of sensibility," and thus "The task of the modern educator is not to cut down jungles but to irrigate deserts." He shrewdly reminds us that "a hard heart is no infallible protection against a soft head" (p. 24).

But second, Lewis objects to this doctrine of the subjectivity of man and the relativity of value because it denies any objective reality. He cites his authorities—Augustine, Aristotle, and Thomas Browne—and argues that all the great cultures of the world have held to a belief in objective reality; he refers to the Hindu *Rta* but uses the Chinese *Tao*, "the reality beyond all predicates," as his key concept. The *Tao*, he says, is "the doctrine of objective value, the belief that certain attitudes are really true, and others really false, to the kind of thing the universe is and the kind of things we are" (p. 29).

Lewis the critic is here stalking Reality as steadily as did his character Ransom, first fitfully on Malacandra and then more determinedly on Perelandra. He argues that an educator who is outside the *Tao* is really engaged in producing "men without chests." The chest is the place of "emotions organized by trained habit into stable sentiments" and is the needed link between head and gut: "It may even be said that it is by this middle element that man is man: for by his intellect he is mere spirit and by his appetite mere animal" (p. 34).

Lewis the novelist has always insisted upon the body, even a celebration of the body, and he is outraged that these "men without chests," the men who debunk or despise emotion, are described as Intellectuals. It was the Devil on Perelandra who wanted to lead us to a belief in "pure spirit."

But Lewis the Rationalist tries to find the real basis for the attack on the *Tao* and tries to imagine what the innovators will substitute for the discarded value system. He finds terms such as "biological" or "healthy" used to commend some virtues more than others, but he argues that this makes little sense. "The innovator attacks traditional value [the *Tao*] in defence of what he at first supposes to be (in some special sense) 'rational' or 'biological' values. But as we have seen, all the values which he uses in attacking the *Tao*, and even claims to be substituting for it are themselves derived from the *Tao*" (pp. 53-54). But: "The human mind has no more power of inventing a new value than of imagining a new primary colour, or, indeed, of creating a new sun and a new sky for it to move in" (pp. 56-57).

It might be concluded that Lewis means that man is abolishing himself by refusing to accept the *Tao* or even "the ultimate platitudes of Practical Reason" (p. 61), but the abolition goes deeper and is more specific. It is, in a way, a kind of intellectual "Westonism." Lewis sees the abolition of the *Tao* as a *scientific*, as well as philosophic, premise; and thus, the advances of sciences, so often called "man's conquest of nature," mean really a conquest of man himself. First, like a novelist, he sees that this conquest of nature, "if the dreams of some scientific planners are realized, means the rule of a few hundreds of men over billions upon billions of men" (p. 71). The same novelist, even in this extremely tightly reasoned argument, takes a moment to give us detailed pictures: "But many a mild-eyed scientist in pince-nez, many a popular dramatist, many an amateur philosopher in our midst, means in the long run just the same as the Nazi rulers of Germany" (p. 85).

Lewis envisions a "final stage" of man's conquest of nature in which "Man by eugenics, by pre-natal conditioning, and by an education and propaganda, has obtained full control over himself," and thus "*Human* nature will be the last part of Nature to surrender to Man" (p. 72). And what will the conditioners do with their power? Lewis answers, in effect, that there is quite literally no telling because they have rejected the *Tao* and have thus "stepped into the void"(p. 77). But he argues persuasively that the conditioners won't want any trouble, so that "Nature will be troubled no more by the restive species that rose in revolt against her so many millions of years ago, will be vexed no longer by its chatter of truth and mercy and beauty and happiness" (p. 80).

The conclusion of this book is bluntly simple. After making the point that "We reduce things to mere Nature *in order that* we may 'conquer' them," and that Nature is in fact the very "name for what we have, to some extent, conquered" (pp. 82-83), Lewis sees our taking "the final step of reducing our own species to the level of mere Nature" (p. 83). We cannot have it both ways: we cannot give up and retain the human spirit. So this is the conclusion: "Either we are rational spirit obliged forever to obey the absolute values of the *Tao*, or else we are mere nature to be kneaded and cut into new shapes for the pleasures of masters who must, by hypothesis, have no motive but their own 'natural' impulses" (p. 84).

But there is a coda to this argument. Lewis says, almost parenthetically, that it was a "magician's bargain" by which man surrendered "object after object, and finally himself, to Nature in return for power" (p. 87). In asking for a reconsideration of Science and its powers, Lewis makes the sensible suggestion that we ask for a new, a "regenerative science." Surely he would have been cheered by today's ecologists who ask and insist that science respect at least the earth. Lewis says, "The regenerative science which I have in mind would not do even to minerals and vegetables what modern science threatens to do to man himself" (pp. 89-90). We still need a kind of ecology of man to protect us from the direst conditioning of the behaviorist, of course. But Lewis wonders aloud about the connection between science and magic. It was not the Middle Ages, he says, which produced much magic: "the sixteenth and seventeenth centuries are the high noon of magic" (p. 87). He argues that the scientist and magician, the Bacons and the Fausts, were after power, not knowledge. Modern science, he says, "was born in an unhealthy neighborhood and at an inauspicious hour" (p. 89). The connection between magic and science is as paradoxical as it is tantalizing.

When *The Abolition of Man* was finished, Lewis began, almost immediately, to write *That Hideous Strength* which, since its principal theme is precisely this connection between the old magic and the modern applied science, might be seen as a kind of gigantic footnote to the conclusion of *The Abolition of Man*.

But it is not merely an illustration of Lewis' beliefs. It is not like, say, B. F. Skinner's use of his novel, *Walden Two,* to illustrate his belief in the possibility and desirability of the very social and psychological conditioning to which Lewis was so opposed. (*That Hideous Strength* almost seems to be a brilliant refutation of *Walden Two*—although, of course, Lewis' was the antecedent novel.) *Walden Two* merely illustrates for us, in an enjoyably readable novel, the vision of a perfectly harmonious, perfectly conditioned community, which Skinner envisions in his psychological work.

That Hideous Strength, however, does not merely illustrate Lewis' beliefs (though it does that occasionally): it offers him the only way that he has of exploring the connection between science and magic in the modern world and the ways this connection affects individual humans. The brilliance of the method can be seen in the way Lewis juggles the realistic elements with the fantasy.

The novel recounts the efforts of an extremely large and powerful group called the NICE, the National Institute for Coordinated Experiments, which—as its superbly chosen name suggests—has an excellent public relations department and is not answerable to any existing educational or political institutions. (One of its claims is that it will "cut out the red tape.") It has so much power that one of the most interesting questions in the novel is really about the nature of power: What does anyone want to *do* with that much power? It transpires that the NICE, in addition to using and perfecting every conceivable kind of modern technological power from the subtlest conditioning through the most brutal force, is turning even to magic. The plot turns on the NICE's attempt to find and use the still-alive greatest of all British magicians, Merlin.

Meantime, another, pitifully smaller, group has got wind of these developments and is trying to find and use Merlin for their side. Magic is simply power and can be used for good or ill. This small group turns out to be "Logres" (a concept Lewis borrowed from his friend Charles Williams, as other details, like Numinor, are borrowed from another Inkling, J. R. R. Tolkien), and it is headed by the ever-present "just man," the current "Pendragon" of Logres, Ransom.

Ransom is much changed since his trip back from Perelandra: he is godlike. He has the same wound in his heel, got in his fight with the Devil on Perelandra, and it is still bleeding. Lewis continues one of his favorite themes (also borrowed from Williams): we must fight each other's battles and cure each other's wounds—there is little we can do for ourselves; we need each other in unexpected ways, and we must surrender ourselves in unexpected ways. Among other things, life is simply more *peculiar* than we had thought.

The design of the book is wonderful: the complex plot and great number of characters are kept in line by Lewis' beginning with a single, simple unhappy marriage. The novel opens with Jane Studdock wondering why she, a six-month bride, is so unhappy. Her husband Mark is a don at Bracton College in the small university of Edgestow; he is ambitious, a bit insecure and driven, and inclined to ignore his wife: Lewis makes it clear that their sex life is hopelessly unsatisfactory because they simply pay too little attention to each other. They both suffer from "cold love and feeble trust." Mark is attracted by an offer to join some of his fellow academics at the NICE, while Jane is directed toward the "Company" headed by Ransom because she has been suffering from nightmares that turn out to be visions of reality—in the manner of the dreams in Dunne's *An Experiment with Time*.

Although Lewis will deal with very large issues indeed, he never abandons these two characters and their private, unspectacular griefs. Here too he seems like a typically medieval writer who, like Spenser, quite naturally thought on two or three levels simultaneously. For Lewis, the three levels are the private, the college, and the state. He seems to say that no one of these can be understood without reference to the others. As George Eliot once said, "There is no private life which has not been determined by a wider public life." Lewis tries to show the effect working both ways.

In the background to *That Hideous Strength* is not only *The Abolition of Man* and its argument about the end of the traditional conception of man, there is also the story of the tower of Babel—and what medieval writer would ever write without at least one Biblical reference?—which, in fact, is what is described as possessing "hideous strength." The scientists are unknowingly but pridefully erecting a tower of confusion: the mad confusion of purposes and aims and the resulting deterioration of language is one of the chief themes of the book. The fuzziness of our language, especially of our public or official language, is treated hilariously and seriously: the point is that a culture with dangerous, unexamined, or divisive ideas; a culture with no common education or values or premises; a culture that does not value as sacred or at least inviolable the rights of the individual is a culture which is doomed. And its doom is seen first, as in the Biblical story, in a gross deterioration of language: people cannot understand each other.

Lewis studies this theme on three levels. The collapse of the tower of Babel the NICE has constructed at Belbury is the great and fantastic climax of the novel. At the college level, the deterioration of language is merely manipulative: no one, not even C. P. Snow, has shown so well the subtleties of college politics: the brilliant account of the college meeting (pp. 22-28) is a superb rehearsal—as it were—for the collapse of the NICE at Belbury (pp. 343-58).

But Lewis is always chiefly interested in the individual soul—especially in those people who deny the existence of this soul. The Deputy Director (though called Deputy, he really runs the place—of course) is Mr. Wither, a man of baffling and endless verbiage who can hardly be understood any more than one can actually hear music in Muzak. Mr. Wither (and the type he represents has positively flowered since World War II in politics, business, education, everywhere), when asked a direct question becomes mild, gentle, faraway. When Mark Studdock asks him what his duties will be at the NICE, Mr. Wither responds, first by genially assuring him there will not be "the smallest difficulty" (a favorite Wither phrase) on that point. "There was never any idea of circumscribing your activities and your general influence on policy, much less your relations with your colleagues and what I might call in general the terms of reference under which you would be collaborating with us, without the fullest possible consideration of your own views and, indeed, your own advice" (pp. 52-53). And so on . . . and on . . . and on. Poor Mark never finds out what he is supposed to do. (Actually, it transpires that the NICE really wants *Jane* Studdock for her psychic powers.)

Wither is one of the conditioners who seems to have sprung to fictional life from *The Abolition of Man*: he has pursued power in the modern mode, softly, quietly, verbosely. For Lewis, it is as—probably more—important that one understand the single soul of John Wither than it is even to understand what Wither represents. Of course, what he represents is precisely what he has chosen for himself. When, in the end, he knows he has lost everything, "It is incredible how little this knowledge moved him." Why? Because he is a Conditioner: "Because he had long ceased to believe in knowledge itself." He has become a kind of Gothic monster of Subjectivity: in him is a "fixed refusal of everything that was in any degree other than himself." Lewis is precise: Wither went through Hegel, Hume, Pragmatism, Logical Positivism and at last (in a phrase common to both *The Abolition of Man* and the novel) "into the complete void." Yet Wither is responsible: "He had willed with his whole heart that there should be no reality and no truth." Perhaps there is a moment when reality could become objective to him, "but he cannot make the knowledge real to himself" (p. 353).

The theme of knowledge as Reality has, in addition to its moral significance for the individual characters, an ironic dimension: Lewis pictures scientist after scientist in this novel who knows not quite what he is doing.

The other principal characters in the NICE include a clergyman who is something of a modern, materialistic version of the nineteenth century's "muscular Christian": he insists that the Kingdom of Heaven is—despite what Jesus had to say on the subject—to be realized on Earth. He believes that the doctrine of the Resurrection of the Body is a materialistic, even grossly materialistic, matter, and in the end he adores the horror-film "Head" of the NICE. In a sense, all the characters—like Weston on Perelandra—choose death rather than life: there is a willed separation of soul and body. Indeed, one NICE employee, named Frost, has become such a thoroughgoing materialist that, quite logically, he doubts his own existence: "His mind was a mere spectator. He could not understand why that spectator should exist at all. He resented its existence, even while assuring himself that resentment also was merely a chemical phenomenon . . . . How infuriating that the body should have power thus to project a phantom self!" (p. 357). His colleague Filostrato is working very directly for the abolition of man—more precisely man's body: Filostrato, like a Creative Evolutionist, wants only Mind: he thinks all organic life is messy, disgusting; he is pleased to note that "six out of ten" English women are frigid because "There will never be peace and order and discipline so long as there is sex" (p. 173). He is quite consistent to the end: his end is his own murder and he remains the observing scientist to the end: "His last thought was that he had underestimated the terror" (p. 355).

Most of these extraordinary characters seem suggested by Lewis' description of the "masters" in *The Abolition of Man*—even the "popular dramatist" from the *Abolition* puts in an appearance as Jules, the novelist and titular Director of the NICE. Moreover, Lewis' assertion that people with only ideas and no apparent power or influence can have devastating effects is taken right from the *Abolition* and made powerful in the novel. In Curry and Busby, two fussy administrators from Bracton College, Lewis has created amusing modern and educational equivalents of Disraeli's famous political hacks, Tadpole and Taper; but he has also created reminders that even fools have consequences. At the end, one of the characters asks, "Was there a single doctrine practised at Belbury which hadn't been preached by some lecturer at Edgestow? Oh, of course, they never thought any one would *act* on their theories!" (p. 371).

Lewis makes Mark Studdock a victim of his own education—not classical, not scientific, but merely "Modern" (p. 185). This is why it is so difficult for him to find Reality: everything about him— his education, his mind, his personality, his very soul—is all so vague. He is a social scientist, a sociologist, one of those who has taken part (without quite knowing it) in the degeneration of science into the "magician's bargain," which Lewis described in *The Abolition of Man*, of exchanging the soul (that is, reality, objective knowledge, the self) for power (even if the power is the mere brutality of Fairy Hardcastle, the policewoman). "Despair of objective truth had been increasingly insinuated into the scientists" (p. 203), and this despair has become the vagueness of the young men like Studdock. As a consequence, he has really only one ambition, to become part of the inner circle, or inner ring, of power, an elusive ambition because one has such difficulty recognizing where the real power is—especially in institutions like colleges or huge bureaucracies. The individual progress of Mark Studdock, from his spaniel desire to please and be accepted to his place at his wife's side at the end, is one of the great developments in the novel. Mark Studdock is in search of the Real—which takes the first simple desire for the normal and then for his wife: she becomes a kind of Reality principle for him.

But Mark Studdock's moral progress is not really so extraordinary in itself. His wife is a different case. She has a different set of assumptions—she wants to be left alone, to call her soul her own, as much as he wants to be part of the inner rings—and her progress to Reality and Selfhood takes the form of her introduction to a particular man. She is a visionary who hates her visions: "But I don't *want* it . . . . I must stop it. I hate this sort of thing . . . . I want to lead an ordinary life. I want to do my own work" (p. 66). The account of her conversion (pp. 314-19) is as fascinating and absorbing as anything Lewis ever wrote, a process which begins with her simply *seeing* the godlike Ransom—"Jane looked; and instantly her world was unmade" (p. 142)—an approach which insists on how *personal* is Christianity. Her later conversion to Christianity is attended by the awareness of Reality: indeed, many things make sense to her that never did before; the world has become more beautiful, meaningful, more highly charged: and since the novel ends with a kind of gigantic sexual dance—Venus has drawn near the earth, and Ransom will be leaving forever—the novel's close, with its preparation for the love-making of Mark and Jane, suggests that even Paganism is absorbed into, and become part of, the Christian experience. One of Lewis' favorite themes is that everything is clearer to the Christian.

However, Mark and Jane's progress from "cold love and feeble trust" to the full richness of personality, reality, sex and love is not the main business of the novel. What is most interesting about the novel is precisely that it is not. If it were, the novel would have been structured dramatically like so many science-fiction/ fantasy attacks on the modern soulless state. The most famous of such attacks, *Brave New World* and *1984*, posit an enemy that has much in common with the NICE—particularly Huxley's, with his picture of the perfect conditioning that biology gives the state. The dramatic opposition to the smooth, perfectly conditioned, state-organized society of *Brave New World* is an individual, the Savage. This is a Romantic opposition; not surprisingly, our general attitude toward the individual and "society" since the French Revolution has been fairly explicitly one of opposition. This is partially true because we identify "society" with the "state," and the states in the nineteenth and twentieth centuries have tended to demand the surrender of the self from the citizens. Hegel, one of history's most influential philosophers, said that the State "has the supreme right against the individual, whose supreme duty is to be a member of the State."

However, where Huxley and Orwell imagine a soullessly efficient, all-powerful state, conceived on the Prussian or Hegelian model, Lewis' NICE is more whimsical, more capricious and, despite the elements of overt fantasy, more plausible. But the main difference is in the kind of response to the totalitarian danger that the State or the NICE represents. Huxley and Orwell naturally imagine Romantic loners, outsiders who, more or less alone, must battle the machine-like efficiency of the State. Strictly speaking, this is a "modern" response because it places the early nineteenth-century's Romantic hero in a modern totalitarian setting and asks him, like Prometheus, to rebel.

Nowhere is the medieval cast of Lewis' mind more in evidence than in the *kind* of response he imagines. Ransom gathers a company around him: this is Logres, the "just men" who persevere as a sort of very small, very secret society. But the key point is that it is a society within a society, a society within the state, a society which is something almost unimaginable in the modern consciousness—a society which is an *alternative* to the state. (Ordinarily, in the modern world, societies within the state are, or are seen to be, even more dangerous than the state itself—from the real SS of Hitler to the fictional police force in the film *Magnum Force*.)

Long before Jane Studdock becomes a Christian, she becomes a member of this bizarre company. Only later can her marriage work—because marriage, we are reminded on the opening page of the novel, was ordained for "mutual society, help and comfort"— since she has learned from the Company what those words really mean. But at the beginning she is naturally unclear about the society. Of course, a reader would recognize simply the difference in the connotations of the names Lewis has given his characters. The NICE people have harsh-sounding names like Wither, Straik, Frost, Hardcastle—even Devine, our old friend, now devoted even more fully to power, has become Lord Feverstone. The Company has its allegorically named Ransom followed by Professor and Mrs. Dimble, Grace Ironwood, a rationalist and skeptic named MacPhee, Ivy Maggs, Arthur and Camilla Denniston, and two animals—a jackdaw named Baron Corvo (a fascinating choice) and a magnificent bear named Mr. Bultitude. Ransom has an Arthurian pseudonym for a time, Mr. Fisher-King, obviously because of the wound in his heel—which can be cured only on Perelandra.

The Company is based, medieval fashion, on promises made personally to the Head, Ransom. After that, it is weirdly democratic in the way that a highly structured, very personal society can be. Jane is surprised to see her erstwhile servant, Ivy Maggs, treated as a real equal, not with the spurious equality of modern Britain. All take turns working in the kitchen, but there are complex layers and orders. "Equality is not the deepest thing, you know," Ransom tells Jane rather persuasively, because there are so many other things as well (p. 148). Here there is no inner ring because the sacred worth of the individual soul is always insisted upon (p. 168).

Each individual has something to contribute. Nowhere is there a more splendid illustration of E. M. Forster's famous injunction, "Only connect!" than in the Company and the way it deals with the horrors of the NICE. Each has something to contribute, and each contribution is valued in an oddly impersonal way: Ransom makes it clear throughout that he did not choose anyone, that the Company simply formed itself. The point is like the arbitrariness of Ransom's being kidnapped and taken to Malacandra, the adventure which began the whole trilogy: it was whim and it was destiny at the same time. But always one is free to choose (p. 115). Jane's visions, MacPhee's skepticism, Professor Dimble's languages—everyone has something to offer. "Only connect" applies also to the animals: Mr. Bultitude has a magnificent moment to himself, and all the animals join in the great final dance of sexual love.

After the bears go off to mate and the jackdaw Baron Corvo begins a love affair, a stallion is heard whinnying in the garden. MacPhee says, "This is becoming indecent." " 'On the contrary,' said Ransom, 'decent, in the old sense, *decens*, fitting, is just what it is. Venus herself is over St. Anne's' " (p. 376). A bit later Shakespeare's famous line,"She comes nearer the Earth than she was wont, to make men mad," is altered to, "She comes more near the Earth than she was wont to—to make Earth sane" (p. 378).

Exactly. The goddess of love is needed not to make us mad—ambition, fear, selfishness and power will do that—but to make us sane. Life is a call to battle; but, without love, power becomes hideous. With love, things fall into place. Ransom says, "Perelandra [Venus] is all about us and Man is no longer isolated. We are now as we ought to be—between the angels who are our elder brothers and the beasts who are our jesters, servants and playfellows" (p. 378). When Ransom tells Jane, "Go in obedience and you will find love," he means that obedience is the recognition of place and order (pp. 379-80). Without a nervous insistence upon the self, the real selves are found, and the end of the novel shows the transfiguration of the characters: the women become love goddesses, the men become gallant lovers. The call to battle has become the call to joy.

Strength is always needed, of course: the raising of Merlin—and the creation of Merlin in all his amusing and revealing totality is among the greatest of Lewis' technical accomplishments—requires strength and knowledge. Merlin is power, but the novel dramatizes what Lewis had insisted upon in *The Abolition of Man*: the use of power must not be separated from a prior consideration of the value of that power.

When that separation occurs, there is an entirely new conception of power. And here *That Hideous Strength* becomes subtly medieval in effect: the medieval writers rarely wrote explicitly about the present (it was often dangerous to do so), but the present rather seeped into the work. So with Lewis. The novel was written during World War II—although at first it seems to have nothing whatever to do with the war. But Lewis has shown, subtly though powerfully, what happens when power no longer serves even the needs of the all-powerful Hegelian state. Lewis may have anticipated the behaviorist triumphs in psychology, but in sketching what happens to power, he was really describing the fascist present. Indeed, Lewis makes Fairy Hardcastle say, "*Of course* we're non-political. The real power always is" (p. 99).

Like Hitler, the members of the NICE despise those messy, compromising politicians. In the end, the NICE is simply the adoration of the *idea* of power.

It is almost too depressing to point out that Lewis' attack on psychological conditioning is still as relevant and pointed as is his deeper analysis of the horror of power disjoined from any value, its hideous strength.

VII

LAST WORKS: "FURTHER IN AND HIGHER UP"

In the last decade or so of his life, Lewis seems to have seen God less clearly, perhaps even less surely, but more profoundly, more passionately. It is apparently not true that religious belief becomes necessarily more certain the longer it is held. Certainly for writers as deeply religious as Lewis or Graham Greene, the ways of God grow progressively more puzzling; and the glass becomes, if anything, darker.

W. H. Auden said that Melville at the end of his life, "sailed into a great mildness." That is exactly what Lewis did not do. One might have expected that his writing of *That Hideous Strength* meant he had "found himself" as a writer; and *The Great Divorce*, published in the same year, 1945, suggests that he could have gone on writing barbed satire, rather in the manner of a William Buckley or an Evelyn Waugh, from an enviably secure theological and philosophical position.

It is true that his scholarship, his critical writing as well as his non-fiction religious writing all became, in his last decade, more brilliant, more exact, more consistently interesting and precise. But his fiction, strangely, shows signs of being troubled, disturbed. Instead of going on along the lines of *That Hideous Strength*, Lewis immersed himself in a long series of children's books. "In my end is my beginning": these children's books, the seven Chronicles of Narnia, obviously fulfill the implied promise of his first stories, the "Boxen" stories written with his brother. They also contain, in addition to some of the best writing ever executed for children, some moving theological speculation.

At the same time, through the early 1950s, that Lewis worked on the seven Chronicles of Narnia, he also continued his scholarly work, exploring, with exquisite detail, the connections between

71

the Middle Ages and the Renaissance. Everything about his critical work at this time shows a wisdom and calm strength that comes from a strenuously achieved knowledge.

But his last novel, *Till We Have Faces* (1956), is no obvious summing up: it is a difficult, rather strange novel, whose comparative failure distressed Lewis because he thought it his best book. Even today, *Till We Have Faces* has a special place in Lewis' work: the object of either extravagant praise or silent neglect, the novel has an oddly tentative quality—as if it should have been the first, and experimental, novel of Lewis' "last" period. Alas, there was no final period; but "Old men should be explorers," and Lewis explored wonderingly in this difficult novel. The novel is a myth, that of Cupid and Psyche, re-told—a myth, Lewis said, that had haunted him from his adolescence. In all these last works, Lewis explored deeply his own past, his own deepest dreams, and his own deeply hidden images of God. In many ways, the theme of a hidden God works its way through all the late works.

Both the first of the Narnian Chronicles and *Till We Have Faces* begin with, in effect, complaints against God for being hidden: Orual, the main character of *Till We Have Faces*, draws up a formal charge against the gods; she cannot know that she is living at the end of an era: the novel is set in one of the non-Hellenic lands between the end of the Golden Age of Athens and the birth of Christ. Lucy, the first of the children to enter Narnia, finds herself in a country where it is always winter but never Christmas.

Both works begin in darkness, and we watch the struggles of Lewis' characters to fight their way through to the light. In *The Lion, the Witch and the Wardrobe*, the first of the Narnia Chronicles, the children go through a dark, musty wardrobe. It is a very ordinary household appurtenance, this wardrobe, but it turns out to be the gateway to a land of enchantment, or, rather, not an enchanted land but a land where enchantment is possible.

Surely a great children's story is not merely a story written for children or a story merely with children as characters; rather, it is a story that presents a world with the crust of routine, or experience, or cynicism rubbed away, so that the reader can recapture some of his or her Edenic delight in seeing the world afresh, as if for the first time. One of Lewis' favorite themes, in fact, is that we have trouble actually seeing our world: weighed down and blinkered by the natural, we miss the supernatural.

The source of our problems, our Original Sin, in fact, is precisely this: we miss the world's glories and realities (and thus even its true miseries) because we don't trust enough. *The Lion The Witch and the Wardrobe* is all about trust. The essence of the plot is trust: the other children do not believe Lucy when she tells them that she has gone through the wardrobe into this land called Narnia. When Edmund does in fact enter Narnia, he lies about it because he wants the other, older, children to think that he is very grown-up; he does not trust them to like him as he is. From this lack of trust, there buds a nastiness that blossoms into a terrible betrayal. Edmund betrays his friends to the wicked White Witch: he thinks, absurdly, that she likes him better than his friends do and that she will do nicer things for him. She merely makes promises; she does not ask for trust.

The children and the Narnians can progress from the dead, birthless winter to the crocuses of spring only by means of blood: the great lion Aslan agrees to die, slain by the witch, to save Edmund (and, by extension, the other children and all the talking beasts in Narnia). The witch is quite sure that with Aslan dead she can rule absolutely. She knows that Aslan must keep his promise and must really die: she knows, as do the Pagan priests in *Till We Have Faces*, a great deal about betrayal and sacrifice and the movements of the earth; but she does not know everything. She does not know about the deeper magic from before the dawn of time—that is, in the realm of the eternal pure spirit—by which Aslan undergoes the great miracle of rebirth. When he is reborn, Narnia can be saved at last; with Aslan's blood on the ground, the land can blossom into spring.

But always there is a price to be paid: even the spring itself, with its growth and warmth, means struggle. And the rest of the Narnia Chronicles record some of the struggles that Aslan's land goes through: it closes (in a reminiscence of *Out of the Silent Planet*) with the end of Narnia, and the penultimate volume, *The Magician's Nephew*, gives us an account of the creation of Narnia and the gift of speech to its animals. Certainly one of Lewis' greatest achievements is the sheer size of his vast creation: we learn about Narnia from beginning to end; and we learn of a world which is both logical and alogical, a world with almost Wagnerian echoes (Aslan cannot, like Wotan, break his own laws), a world that is convincingly cosmic and homely, awesome and funny, peopled with awesomely mythical creatures like the centaurs and simply great "faery" creations, such as the aristocratic mouse Reepicheep.

Lewis' own style developed rapidly. In *The Lion, the Witch and the Wardrobe*, Lewis' tone is a bit self-consciously avuncular, even the slightest bit condescending. But by the second story, *Prince Caspian*, he has an assured and simple narrative tone which becomes, by the end of the Chronicles, a genuinely noble and serious "high" style—almost a development of and improvement on the style William Morris (one of Lewis' heroes) adopted for his romances. Here is convincingly "faery" dialogue, reeking of old battles and ancient courtesy: Tirian, in *The Last Battle*, says, "I have done thee some discourtesy, soldier . . . but such was my need. If we meet again I may happen to do thee a better turn." Then Tirian approaches his noble war-horse: "He put his left arm round the beast's neck and bent and kissed its nose and both had great joy" (p. 62).

Although *Prince Caspian* lacks some of the driving power and resonance of the first story, it is an excellent adventure story about how the true prince of Narnia, Prince Caspian, is aided by the children in his fight to regain Narnia's throne from his evil uncle. The story has sharply defined characters, superb pace, and many brilliantly written individual scenes: indeed, Lewis describes battles so well that we realize our modern writers have not culti-vated this skill—no doubt because most of the real wars in our world tend to be horrible, pointless, and without glory. If *Prince Caspian* does not develop any further Lewis' serious themes, it serves to keep Narnia sufficiently enchanted, and it does de-velop two of Lewis' favorite themes—that we must fight each other's battles and be always ready to hear a magic horn which just might call us to adventure.

These are themes at the center of *The Voyage of the "Dawn Treader,"* the story which comes closest to allegory. It begins with the "conversion" of an odious little boy: the first line tells us, "There once was a boy called Eustace Clarence Scrubb, and he almost deserved it." While the other children help Caspian go to the ends of the world to search for the Seven Lost Lords of Nar-nia, Eustace merely complains. He does most of his complaining in a series of diary entries that are among the most amusing pages in all Lewis: the dreary self-absorption, the constant cultivation of one's grievances and unhappiness, the spiteful meanness, and, most of all, the refusal to accept either a call to battle or a sum-mons to joy—these are all laid out with the skill of a Browning. Much earlier Lewis had made his Screwtape say, "All humans turn into the thing they are pretending to be." Eustace turns into a dragon. But then he repents in his loneliness and rejoins the human race by simply liking and allowing others to like him. Then, to make the conversion manifest, Aslan pulls off his old dragon's skin, and (born again) Eustace becomes a new boy.

Eustace had to learn (as did they all) to trust: without trust, no one could find adventure; with no adventure (even with its possible dangers, its battles, wounds, even deaths—the immortal mouse Reepicheep, for example, disappears, apparently forever, at the end), no one could find Aslan. The closing pages of the novel make the meaning very clear. Aslan tells Edmund and Lucy that they cannot come back to Narnia; they are too old. When they protest that it is him, not only Narnia, they will miss, he explains that they must now move closer to their own (adult) world, wherein he is known by another name. He drives it in: it was to know Him that they were sent into Narnia in the first place.

It was something like the center of a medieval allegory which provided Lewis with the general frame for *The Voyage of the "Dawn Treader"* wherein Narnia represents a child's imagination, which is the source of one's first awareness of God's workings in the world. It was the center of a classical epic that provided a similar frame for *The Silver Chair*, one of the very best of the seven stories. Once more, the plot centers on the rectifying of a past betrayal: Eustace Scrubb with a friend named Jill Pole is sent by Aslan to find the imprisoned Rilian, who is Caspian of Narnia. Guided by the mournfully marvelous Puddleglum, they find the true prince imprisoned in Underland (the Narnian Underworld).

The journey to Underland is like the traditional descent of the epic hero to the Underworld. The children are guided by Four Signs, which are told them by Aslan, who makes them repeat the signs like the sacraments in a catechism: the children have to trust Aslan, literally in the dark, but they are aided throughout their journey by these signs: following them is at once a declaration of loyalty to Aslan and the using of their faith in Aslan to help them on their journey through Narnia.

The children must confront the inhabitants of Underland, who are entirely skeptical that this land above the earth, one illumined by something called the sun, actually exists. The children trying to "prove" the existence of "Overland" is the equivalent of Lewis' own attempts to prove to his skeptical readers the existence of a still higher world, the Supernatual, with its own Son. One of the most interesting and revealing moments in any fiction by Lewis occurs when Puddleglum, frustrated at being unable to "prove" the existence of Overland, cries out that the world he is talking about is so immeasurably greater than this miserable Underland that he will believe in it anyway. Echoing Lewis' deep instinct to preserve the good and fight for even a lost cause, Puddleglum deprecates "this black pit of a kingdom" and says proudly, "I'm on Aslan's side even if there isn't any Aslan to lead it." And he adds, "I'm going to live as much like a Narnian as I can even if there isn't any Narnia" (p. 159).

Narnia itself is the subject of *The Horse and His Boy*, the only story that is set entirely in Narnia. It concludes with a genuinely epic battle and opens with some lovely and amusing exoticism out of the Arabian Nights. And there are more Wagnerian echoes:

the relationship between the young hero Shasta and his "Father" is surely derived from the relationship between Siegfried and Mime. Shasta, accompanied by the Princess Aravis—a wonderful character, who wants much more out of life, more passion and intensity, than most of her friends—and two Talking Horses, Hwin and Bree, is set on a characteristically Lewisian path: in helping Prince Corin save Narnia from invasion, he ends by helping himself: it is revealed that Shasta is really Cor, Prince Cor, the elder twin brother of Corin.

This splendid adventure story culminates in a great battle scene in which Lewis has the chance to develop a modern version of a high epic style. Moreover, he can develop his favorite themes of honor and loyalty. Behind it all, of course, is the matter of loyalty to Aslan, but in this story Aslan takes on a kind of significance he has not had earlier in the Chronicles. First, we are told that one must speak *to* Aslan, and only then can Aslan reveal oneself to oneself—with this proviso: "I tell no one any story but his own." The emphasis, somewhat surprisingly perhaps, is on the individual's working out his own destiny. When asked who he is, Aslan can only say, "Myself"—that is, pure being, pure identity: one might say that Lewis is driving his Chronicles philosophically in a strongly Platonic direction.

Oddly enough, Lewis develops, even delightfully plays with, the Platonic question of the relationship between perceived worlds in *The Magician's Nephew*. Yet formally there could hardly be a stronger contrast between *The Horse and His Boy* and *The Magician's Nephew*. Digory, the nephew of the magician, goes into Narnia from a nostaligically conceived Victorian London, and the comings and goings between the two worlds are unusually intricate: this is the only story in which there is a return to England in the middle, and the villainous witch has a partly horrific and partly comic time in this strange "real" world.

It is appropriate that it should be so, for in *The Magician's Nephew* Lewis takes as his subject the creation of Narnia. (If one were to read the stories, not in the order in which Lewis wrote them but rather in a straight chronological order, this story would be first, and the concluding story, *The Last Battle*, last.) In many ways, this is the subtlest, most delicate of all the Chronicles. The witch is a great study in evil, but her megalomania is all the more powerful because it sets up echoes in Digory's mind: the witch reminds him of his uncle, and the other characters recall their other lives as if they were dreams.

Lewis' re-telling of the creation myth is powerful because it contains a brilliant account of creation ("a grassy land bubbling like a pot of water" [p. 113] as well as the astute point that not everyone can so much as see the creation. Aslan's first command to Narnia is "Awake!" Then follow: Love, Think, Speak (p. 116). Aslan, pure being himself, says, "I give you yourselves" (p. 118). Lacking trust, Uncle Andrew can see none of this: instead of the miracle of the creation of the Talking Beasts, he sees, fearfully, only a pack of wild animals. "For what you see and hear depends a good deal on where you are standing: it also depends on what sort of person you are" (p. 125).

If Lewis has not given us a quite new creation myth, he has re-told the creation story in Genesis with an affecting and revealing combination of the cosmic and the personal. It is in a Garden (Narnia's Eden) that the witch tempts Digory with knowledge, and the children must remember Aslan's warnings that an evil might infect Narnia—such as the Deplorable Word, which is as destructive as the Bomb—or any means of self-destruction that humans or Talking Beasts can devise. The Narnian tree planted in England and chopped down to make the magic wardrobe is a characteristic touch: it helps to make this children's story as powerful as *Perelandra* (which it resembles) and helps to give coherence to all the other Chronicles of Narnia.

Of all the Chronicles, the final work, *The Last Battle*, is the most unashamedly allegorical. Like the first of the Space Trilogy, *The Last Battle* is the most eschatological: its subject is the end of Narnia.

In the final days of Narnia, a false Aslan has been devised by a clever ape. Confusion reigns; but even after the false Aslan has been exposed, by the last King, Tirian, aided by the children Eustace Scrubb and Jill Pole, the effects of the deception go on: the lack of trust is clearest among the Dwarfs. Having been taken in by the false Aslan, they cannot believe in the true one. They cannot trust the general or "common" knowledge Lewis always put such stock in; they cannot take "the adventure that comes to us" (p. 20); they are cynical and cunning; and—like Wagner's Nibelungs or modern wage slaves—they are taught to believe in "true freedom," which turns out to mean "doing what I tell you" (p. 31).

The final battle is, of course, a call to adventure and possible death; it also depends upon knowledge and trust to overcome "fear and hatred" (p. 153). Guided by the cry of "further in and higher up" (p. 154), the children and King Tirian must accept the end of Narnia, must learn exactly in what senses Tash—the evil spirit of Narnia—and Aslan can be the same (p. 165), must find a new Narnia where "the inside is larger than the outside" (p. 180).

In the end, the children have "died" in their real, English, world as well as in the Narnia they understood as children: but all that is now "the Shadow-Lands" (p. 183). In a strikingly Platonic eternal world, the children and the Narnians "live happily ever after" in their new life "which was only the beginning of the real story" (p. 184).

The single great paradoxical truth about this whole series of children's fantasies is that it has all been concerned with one object—the search for the real. And that search, very exactly, is the subject of Lewis' last novel, *Till We Have Faces*.

Lewis clearly wants this book to attempt an answer to the most difficult of all questions for a religious quester: Why does God hide himself from us? Why is it that we must be tortured by hints of God's existence, vaguely feel that the world is not exactly as it appears to us, feel the spark of the divine in our very blood and hearts and, yet, finally and maddeningly, not be able to see God in the face?

It is small wonder that Lewis was "haunted" from adolescence by the myth of Psyche and Eros, the re-telling of which gave him the means to begin an answer to these questions. It is precisely this story, especially when it is seen as the culmination of Paganism and the prefiguring of Christianity, which connects humans and the gods in love.

In the account of the myth from Apuleius, Psyche's great beauty caused her to be left, owing to the jealousy of Venus, on a mountain, prey to a dragon. But she was seen by Cupid (Eros) who fell in love with her, kept her in a palace, and made love to her at night but forbade her ever to look on his face. When she asked that she might be visited by her sisters, the god agreed; but the sisters felt envy and persuaded Psyche that her mysterious lover was a monster whom she must kill: they give her a lamp and a knife for the purpose. However, when Psyche lit her lamp and gazed upon the beauty of the sleeping god, she could not kill him. But a drop of oil from the lamp woke him: reproaching her, he disappears, leaving her to the cruel twists of fate devised by the envious Venus.

The great change in Lewis' version is that the sisters are not consumed with malice when they see Psyche's great happiness: rather, they cannot see it at all; for them, the palace, the god, love itself are invisible (just as Uncle Andrew could not see the creation of Narnia). One must learn to see the face of the god.

Lewis characterizes the two sisters sharply. One, Redival, is a silly, chattering girl who does indeed envy Psyche's beauty. The other, Orual, is so ugly that she must hide her face behind a veil; but she loves Psyche. Psyche is not only beautiful; she seems to be love itself. Orual has a different road to take: she becomes a warrior and a great Queen, inheriting their father's relatively minor kingdom.

The novel is told, in a brilliantly imagined historical reconstruction, in the first person from Orual's point of view. The story of Psyche and especially of her sacrifice is told as powerfully as the myth itself and as excitingly as *King Kong* (which at times it almost resembles). It is given resonance and depth by being cast in the form of a charge against the gods. Orual has seen far too much to doubt the existence of the gods, and she is dutifully and fearfully respectful of the local goddess Ungit, who represents, roughly, the dark forces of the earth. Free from fear, as she says at the beginning, she challenges the gods to explain how they can give us love and capriciously take it away. She has suffered so much that she concludes that there must be "something great in the mortal soul": "For suffering, it seems, is infinite, and our capacity without limit" (p. 277).

That capacity for an almost transcendental suffering is the source of Orual's quest for love and knowledge. She is "wandering between two worlds"—between the hard, rather cruel world of her own kingdom (her father thinks nothing of castrating a young man for paying too much attention to Redival; and their goddess Ungit demands blood sacrifice) and the world of the Greeks represented by her tutor and closest friend, known, because of his cunning intelligence, as the Fox. Lewis studied the Greeks all his life, and his creation of a rational Greek in a primitive, superstitious land is among his finest achievements; but he is careful to show that Orual learns the limitations of a purely rational view of the world. The Fox teaches Orual that all must be according to Nature and Reason, that life can be understood in purely rational terms.

It is from Psyche that Orual learns "that the Fox hasn't the whole truth. Oh, he has much of it. It'd be as dark as a dungeon within me but for his teaching. And yet . . . I can't say it properly. He calls the whole world a city. But what's a city built on? There's earth beneath. And outside the wall?" (pp. 70-71).

From her own dreams, from her studies with the Fox, and from her love for Psyche, Orual learns. She sees the consolations of philosophy crumble when the Fox weeps at Psyche's presumed death (in a charming echo of the scene with the philosopher in *Rasselas*). With Psyche, she feels that her soul is called to joy, but she is living in a "god-haunted, plague-breeding, decaying, tyrannous world" (p. 97).

It is a profound love that she craves, and Orual knows that Psyche's love for her god means, in one way or another, that she will lose Psyche: "The emptiness of my life was to begin at once"

(p. 99). When she hears Psyche's story—that she was not raped by a monster but loved by a god—she realizes the overwhelming significance of it all: "You have told me so many wonders. If this is true, I've been wrong all my life. Everything has to be begun over again" (p. 115)

It is small wonder that John Donne, in his famous sonnet, had asked God to "ravish" him: Psyche was fortunate enough to have ben loved sexually by a god; there was no doubt, the love was the proof. But Orual, when faced with that palace of love, can see nothing at all. Part of her knows that Psyche tells the truth, but it is all too frightening and mysterious; the implications are too overwhelming, and, whether Psyche tells the truth or is mad, Orual felt "the whole world (Psyche with it) slipping out of my hands" (p. 118).

After this central passage, the rest of the novel is concerned with what Orual can believe. Can she trust enough and love enough to believe the apparent impossibility of Psyche's story? Will she continue to believe in Ungit and the earth-gods? Will she believe in the anti-superstitious rationality of the Fox?

The rest of the novel is concerned with Orual's fate—not Psyche's. This is the most brilliant part, really, of Lewis' conception. For Orual "takes the adventure that comes to her" and proceeds to live her life as best she can. She becomes a warrior-queen, loving no man but enjoying the profound and loving friendship of Bardia, a fellow soldier; she must fight a great single combat to establish her right to rule, and she becomes a just and good Queen. In other words, she becomes herself—with no apparent answer to her questions. But the living of her life in fact constitutes the answer.

The final section of the novel concerns a dream she has in which she at last presents her charge to the gods. "They gave me nothing in the world to love but Psyche and then took her from me . . . . I say the gods deal very unrightly with us. For they will neither (which would be best of all) go away and leave us to live our own short days to ourselves, nor will they show themselves openly and tell us what they would have us do . . . . Why must holy places be dark places?" (p. 249)

This puts the matter abstractly, philosophically. But the most fascinating part of the novel is the transformation of this abstract charge against the gods into a personally felt, the *real* charge. In her dream, Orual says to the gods: "Did you ever remember whose the girl was? She was mine. *Mine*. You're thieves, seducers. That's my wrong. I'll not complain (not now) that you're blood-drinkers and man-eaters" (p. 292).

As Orual hears herself put the charge to the gods, she has her anwer. "The complaint was the answer" (p. 294). Not only does Orual realize how self-absorbed and merely possessive her love for Psyche has been, not only does she realize that her own free life contradicts the possessiveness of the love she has harbored, she understands it all: "I saw well why the gods do not speak to us openly, nor let us answer. Till that word can be dug out of us, why should they hear the babble that we think we mean? How can they meet us face to face till we have faces?" (p. 294).

This is an answer that is as powerful (and, for the novel, as powerfully conclusive) as it is troubling. Throughout the novel, Lewis develops the theme which has grown increasingly important in his late work—that we must follow the god within us. Finally, *Till We Have Faces* tells us that we cannot see God (or the gods) clearly any more than a child could understand the bawdy in Chaucer or the sexual ecstasies of *Tristan*. Through all his work, but especially these last works, Lewis says that life is a preparation—not, as William Butler Yeats said, a preparation for something that never happens—but a readying for seeing God.

In the last analysis, the single virtue that may be most impressive about Lewis as an artist is his courage. All of his work constitutes the only really powerful answer that has been made to the famous argument Joseph Wood Krutch developed in "The Paradox of Humanism" (from *The Modern Temper*)—that as we develop our specifically humanistic qualities, our reason, we become weak. Lewis argues for the assertion of the whole human being—head, heart and gut; and, indeed, sees the heart as the crucial link between the other two. Without love (and its corollaries, loyalty and trust), we cannot hope to see the gods even dimly.

Perhaps of all Lewis' works, the *Chronicles of Narnia* will last longest and be read most deeply. What is most significant and revealing about the fact that even non-Christians want their children to read the Chronicles—an important matter: this giving of the first real books to children!—is not necessarily that they want their children to learn about Christ by analogy with Aslan but rather that the books contain feelings, values, and ways of thought that are so valuable and basic that we want them learned early by children. This may well be Lewis' most profound accomplishment—to transmit to children the things we think are initially, basically, elementally important, interesting, and beautiful. How could any writer ever hope to do more?

VIII

ANNOTATED PRIMARY BIBLIOGRAPHY: FICTION & POETRY
(Page numbers within the text refer to the last cited edition.)

The Dark Tower and Other Stories. Ed. Walter Hooper. New York: Harcourt Brace Jovanovich, 1977. Contains four stories—"The Man Born Blind," "The Shoddy Lands," "Ministering Angels," "Forms of Things Unknown,"—and two fragments of unfinished novels.

Dymer [under the pseudonym of Clive Hamilton]. London: Dent, 1926. A narrative poem, republished in 1950 under Lewis' name with a new Preface in which he summarized the subject of the poem as "the story of a man who, on some mysterious bride begets a monster: which monster, as soon as it has killed its father, becomes a god." Included in *Narrative Poems*, ed. Walter Hooper (see below).

The Horse and His Boy. London: Geoffrey Bles, 1954; rpt. New York: Collier Books, 1970. The Chronicles of Narnia V. The only story set entirely in Narnia. Shasta, aided by the Princess Aravis and two Talking Horses (Hwin and Bree), helps Prince Corin save Narnia from invasion. It transpires that Shasta is really Prince Cor, the elder twin brother of Corin.

The Last Battle. London: The Bodley Head, 1956; rpt. New York: Collier Books, 1970. The Chronicles of Narnia VII. The final story: in the last days, a clever ape has constructed a false Aslan. Even after Jill Pole and Eustace Scrubb help Tirian to expose the deception, confusion reigns. The children die in a railway accident in England at the same time that Narnia ends. The children go on to find a new Narnia where "the inside is larger than the outside."

The Lion, the Witch and the Wardrobe. London: Geoffrey Bles, 1950; rpt. New York: Collier Books, 1970. The Chronicles of Narnia I. Four English children (Peter, Susan, Edmund, and

Lucy) accidentally discover a magic land that lies beyond and through an ordinary wardrobe. In this land, called Narnia, one of them, Edmund, betrays his friends to the wicked White Witch, who has been holding all Narnia in thrall to winter. Only when the lion Aslan agrees to die at the witch's hand can the betrayal be forgiven and Spring come to Narnia.

The Magician's Nephew. London: The Bodley Head, 1955; rpt. New York: Collier Books, 1970. The Chronicles of Narnia VI. Beginning in Victorian London, two children named Polly and Digory—whose Uncle Andrew is a magician—go to Narnia where they meet a Queen who wants magic for power. They are present at the creation of Narnia, when Aslan gives the gift of speech to the animals.

Narrative Poems. Ed. Walter Hooper. New York: Harcourt Brace Jovanovich, 1972. Contains four poems: *Dymer* (with Lewis' 1950 Preface), *Launcelot*, *The Nameless Isle*, *The Queen of Drum*.

Out of the Silent Planet. London: John Lane, 1938; rpt. New York: Macmillan Paperbacks Edition, 1965. First novel of the Space Trilogy. The main character, Ransom, is kidnapped and taken to Malacandra (Mars) as a kind of human sacrifice. Ransom escapes his captors and discovers the inhabitants are friendly. This voyage of philosophical adventure culminates in a trial scene between Ransom and his former captors.

Perelandra. London: John Lane, 1943; rpt. New York: Macmillan Paperbacks Edition, 1965. Second novel of the Space Trilogy. Ransom travels to Perelandra (Venus) where he must fight with the Devil (who has taken possession of Weston, the scientist from the first novel) for the soul of the Green Woman (the Eve of Venus). Ransom succeeds and thus prevents a repetition on Venus of the Earth's fate—the fall and loss of Eden.

The Pilgrim's Regress: An Allegorical Apology for Christianity, Reason and Romanticism. London: Dent, 1933; rpt. Grand Rapids, MI: Eerdmans, 1958. An allegorical account of a search for Joy and Truth; the main character, John, finds these where he least expected them—in a leap of (religious) faith.

Poems. Ed. Walter Hooper. London: Geoffrey Cles, 1964; rpt. New York: Harcourt Brace Jovanovich, 1977. A selection of the poems Lewis wrote all his life. Does not include poems from the first volume, *Spirits in Bondage* (see below).

Prince Caspian: The Return to Narnia. London: Geoffrey Bles, 1951; rpt. New York: Collier Books, 1970. The Chronicles of Narnia II. The four children return to a Narnia much later in time than their last visit. They meet the mouse Reepicheep and all assist Prince Caspian in defeating the Telmarines and bringing back the Old Things.

The Silver Chair. London: Geoffrey Bles, 1953; rpt. New York: Collier Books, 1970. The Chronicles of Narnia IV. Eustace Scrubb, with a friend named Jill Pole, is sent by Aslan to find the imprisoned Rilian—the true Caspian X of Narnia. Guided by Puddleglum, the children help Rilian to escape from Underland.

Spirits in Bondage: A Cycle of Lyrics [under the pseudonym of Clive Hamilton]. London: William Heinemann, 1919. Lewis' first book publication, apparently never reprinted.

That Hideous Strength: A Modern Fairy-Tale for Grown-Ups. London: John Lane, 1945; rpt. New York: Macmillan Paperbacks Edition, 1965. The third novel of the Space Trilogy. Back on Earth, Ransom heads a loosely formed society, Logres, to recall and use Merlin in opposition to the NICE, Lewis' satiric portrait of a modern power-mad bureaucracy. The NICE wants to recondition society but succeeds only constructing a modern Tower of Babel.

Till We Have Faces: A Myth Retold. London: Geoffrey Bles, 1956; rpt. Grand Rapids, MI: Eerdmans, 1966. The story of Cupid and Psyche (how Psyche, a beautiful mortal princess, is loved by Cupid [Eros], the god of love himself and then loses him through a lack of trust) told in the first-person by Orual, one of Psyche's two sisters. Orual learns that we cannot look the gods in the face until we have acquired faces—selves or souls.

The Voyage of the "Dawn Treader." London: Geoffrey Bles, 1952; rpt. New York: Collier Books, 1970. The Chronicles of Narnia III. Edmund and Lucy join their odious cousin Eustace Clarence Scrubb, who becomes an unwilling voyager on a ship with King Caspian. Caspian (and Reepicheep) propose to sail to the World's End. They do. Aslan tells Edmund and Lucy that they are now too old for Narnia and must learn to see him—Aslan—in their own world.

85

IX

PRIMARY BIBLIOGRAPHY: PRINCIPAL NON-FICTION

The Abolition of Man; or, Reflections on Education with Special Reference to the Teaching of English in the Upper Forms of Schools. London: Oxford: Clarendon Press, 1943; rpt. New York: Macmillan Paperbacks Edition, 1965.

The Allegory of Love: A Study in Medieval Tradition. Oxford: Clarendon Press, 1936; rpt. New York: Oxford Paperback, 1958.

The Discarded Image: An Introduction to Medieval and Renaissance Literature. Cambridge: Cambridge University Press, 1964.

English Literature in the Sixteenth Century, excluding Drama. Vol. III: The Oxford History of English Literature. Oxford: Clarendon Press, 1954.

An Experiment in Criticism. Cambridge: Cambridge University Press, 1961.

The Four Loves. London: Geoffrey Bles, 1958.

George MacDonald: An Anthology. London: Geoffrey Bles, 1946.

God in the Dock: Essays on Theology and Ethics. Ed. Walter Hooper. Grand Rapids, MI: Eerdmans, 1970.

The Great Divorce: A Dream. London: Geoffrey Bles, 1946; rpt. New York: Macmillan, 1977.

Letters of C. S. Lewis. Ed. W. H. Lewis. London: Geoffrey Bles, 1966.

Letters to Malcolm: Chiefly on Prayer. London: Geoffrey Bles, 1964.

Miracles: A Preliminary Study. London: Geoffrey Bles, 1947.

Of Other Worlds: Essays and Stories. Ed. Walter Hooper. London: Geoffrey Bles, 1966.

The Problem of Pain. London: Geoffrey Bles, 1940.

Reflections on the Psalms. London: Geoffrey Bles, 1958.

The Screwtape Letters. London: Geoffrey Bles, 1942; rpt.,with

"Screwtape Proposes a Toast" and a new Preface. New York: Macmillan, 1962.

Selected Literary Essays. Ed. Walter Hooper. Cambridge: Cambridge University Press, 1969.

Studies in Words. Cambridge: Cambridge University Press, 1960.

Surprised by Joy: The Shape of My Early Life. London: Geoffrey Bles, 1955; New York: Harcourt Brace, 1955.

X

ANNOTATED SECONDARY BIBLIOGRAPHY

The Lewis scholarship is presently gathering to what will probably be a very considerable crest. Listed below are some of the major books on Lewis: of particular interest to students are the excellent bibliography of Lewis' work by Walter Hooper in *Light on C. S. Lewis* and the invaluable secondary bibliographies in Joe R. Christopher and Joan K. Ostling's *Checklist*, both listed below. *CSL: The Bulletin of the New York C. S. Lewis Society* (466 Orange St., New Haven, CT, 06511) regularly publishes articles on all phases of Lewis' work and tries to keep track of publications about him.

Adey, Lionel. *C. S. Lewis's "Great War" with Owen Barfield.* Univ. of Victoria, B.C.: ELS Monographs, 1978. An assessment of a dispute about the imaginative faculty—whether it can bring new knowledge (Barfield's position) or not.

Carpenter, Humphrey. *The Inklings: C. S. Lewis, J. R. R. Tolkien, Charles Williams, and Their Friends.* London: Allen & Unwin, 1978. Although centered on Lewis, this "collective biography" is a study of all the men in that famous literary circle. Shows the Inklings against the backdrop of the literary culture of the 1920's and 1930's.

Christopher, Joe R., and Joan K. Ostling. *C. S. Lewis: An Annotated Checklist of Writings about Him and His Works.* Kent, OH: Kent State University Press, [1973]. The Serif Series: No. 30: Bibliographies and Checklists. Extensively annotated.

Como, James T. *C.S. Lewis at the Breakfast Table and Other Reminiscences.* New York: Macmillan, 1979. 24 essays of memoir, anecdote, assessment, and analysis, with an Introduction.

Ford, Paul F. *A Companion to Narnia*. New York: Harper and Row, 1980. An encyclopedia listing characters, themes, Biblical allusions in *The Chronicles of Narnia*.

Gibb, Jocelyn, ed. *Light on C. S. Lewis.* London: Geoffrey Bles, 1965. Nine writers reminisce about Lewis and study him as writer, teacher, scholar, Christian apologist. Contains a useful primary bibliography by Walter Hooper.

Gibson, Evan K. *C. S. Lewis, Spinner of Tales: A Guide to His Fiction*. Grand Rapids, MI: Eerdmans, 1980. A guide for the "ordinary reader" to the "ethical and theological implications" of Lewis' fiction including *The Screwtape Letters* and *The Great Divorce*.

Gilbert, Douglas, and Clyde S. Kilby. *C.S. Lewis: Images of His World*. Grand Rapids, MI: Eermans, 1973. Beautiful photographs of Lewis' "world"—Oxford and Cambridge, his home, the English countryside, the sea, Ireland. With a concise biography and study of his religious development.

Green, Roger Lancelyn. *Into Other Worlds: Space-Flight in Fiction, from Lucian to Lewis*. New York: Arno Press, 1975. Historical survey of the subject, wide-ranging. Considerable emphasis on Lewis.

————, and Walter Hooper. *C.S. Lewis: A Biography*. New York: Harcourt Brace Jovanovich, 1974. The "authorized" biography by two of his friends and his literary editor (Hooper). Based on a thorough knowledge of Lewis' work and his friends as well as personal, even intimate, friendships.

Hannay, Margaret Patterson. *C. S. Lewis*. New York: Ungar, 1981. Contains a brief biography followed by summaries of Lewis' novels and critical analyses with a study of Lewis' literary criticism, Christian apologetics, and final works.

Holmer, Paul L. *C.S. Lewis: The Shape of His Faith and Thought.* New York: Harper, 1976. A brief study of Lewis' theology, impact, and critics. Emphasizes the quality of ordinary human knowledge, or "common" knowledge, which informs Lewis' work.

Hooper, Walter. *Past Watchful Dragons: The Narnian Chronicles of C. S. Lewis*. New York: Collier Books, 1979. A study of the development of the creation of Narnia from the life, thought, and temperament of Lewis, written by his biographer.

Howard, Thomas. *The Achievement of C. S. Lewis: A Reading of His Fiction*. Wheaton, Illinois: Harold Shaw Publishers, 1980. A personal and well-received "reading" of the Space Trilogy, *Till We Have Faces*, and the Narnia Chronicles.

Keefe, Carolyn, ed. *C. S. Lewis: Speaker and Teacher*. Grand

Rapids, MI: Zondervan, 1971. Reminiscences by seven people who discuss Lewis the lecturer. Anecdotes and analyses.

Kilby, Clyde S. *The Christian World of C. S. Lewis.* Grand Rapids, MI: Eerdmans, 1964. Pioneering study of Lewis' Christian thought. Emphasis on the fiction and religious writings. Contains a summary of the Chronicles of Narnia.

Kreeft, Peter. *C. S. Lewis: A Critical Essay.* Grand Rapids, MI: Eerdmans, 1969. A pamphlet which emphasizes Lewis' attack on modernism.

Lindskoog, Kathryn Ann. *C. S. Lewis: Mere Christian.* Glendale, CA: Regal Books, 1973. A detailed summary of Lewis' Christian teaching. Contains many cross references to the novels and Narnia Chronicles, as well as to his works of apologetics.

Meilaender, Gilbert. *The Social and Ethical Thought of C. S. Lewis.* Grand Rapids, MI: Eerdmans, 1978. Incorporates all of Lewis' writings into a sustained argument about Lewis' vision of life. Emphasis on Lewis' conception of community.

Reilly, R. J. *Romantic Religion: A Study of Barfield, Lewis, Williams, and Tolkien.* Athens: University of Georgia Press, 1971. Thesis is that Lewis (and the others) defended romanticism by showing it to be religious, and defended religion by "traditionally romantic means." Separate chapters on each writer. The chapter on Lewis emphasizes the fiction, especially *Till We Have Faces.*

Sammons, Martha C. *A Guide through Narnia.* Wheaton, IL: Harold Shaw Publishers, 1979. Biographical sketch, plot outlines of the Chronicles, a study of the geography and history of Narnia, an analysis of the Christian implications, with a glossary.

Schakel, Peter J., ed. *The Longing for a Form: Essays on the Fiction of C. S. Lewis.* Kent, OH: Kent State University Press, 1977. Three general essays on Lewis' fiction, followed by several essays on the Space Trilogy, Chronicles of Narnia, and *Till We Have Faces.*

————. *Reading with the Heart: The Way into Narnia.* Grand Rapids, MI: Eerdmans, 1979. A detailed story-by-story study of the Chronicles which makes use of earlier criticism to help produce an analysis much in the spirit of Lewis' own *Experiment in Criticism.*

Smith, Robert Houston. *Patches of Godlight: The Patterns of Thought of C. S. Lewis.* Athens: The University of Georgia Press, 1981. A study of the underpinnings of Lewis' thought, "his underlying philosophy of religion, as it may be distinguished from his traditional Christian orientation on the one hand and his literary affinities on the other."

Walsh, Chad. *C. S. Lewis: Apostle to the Skeptics*. New York: Macmillan, 1949. Pioneering study of Lewis' importance, his biography, and his work. Surveys the fiction, apologetics, and scholarly work.

_____. *The Literary Legacy of C. S. Lewis*. New York: Harcourt, 1979. With reservations about Lewis' apologetics, the author offers an enthusiastic but balanced evaluation of Lewis' fiction.

White, William Luther. *The Image of Man in C. S. Lewis*. Nashville: Abingdon Press, 1969. Originally a seminary doctoral dissertation, this emphasizes Lewis' importance in twentieth-century Christian culture. Summarizes Lewis' theology; analyzes and refutes Lewis' critics.

INDEX

57720015